WORMW SCRUBS: THE INSIDE STORY

WORMWOOD SCRUBS: THE INSIDE STORY

ANGELA LEVIN

First published in 2014
by GFI&A, 2nd Floor,
167-169 Great Portland Street,
London, W1W 5PF.

ISBN 978-1-5004-4089-3

© 2014 GFI&A

Designed by Martin Colyer

INTRODUCTION

When I first became a member of the watchdog body, the Independent Monitoring Board (IMB), at HM Prison Wormwood Scrubs in west London ten years ago I had no intention of ever writing a book about my experiences. I changed my mind after February 2014 as over the previous months conditions in the Victorian prison had taken a sharp turn for the worse.

The decline began in October 2013, at the start of a new regime that had been announced by the Ministry of Justice about two years earlier. From the start it sounded like one of those unenforceable Government initiatives that looks powerful and impressive on paper but would be extraordinarily difficult to implement in practice.

I had by then got to know and understand the complexities, frustrations and overwhelming bureaucracy of a large prison, and what a challenge it was to run a strict but humane regime for up to 1,279 convicted and remand inmates, plus detainees awaiting deportation.

I realised that changes in procedure and practice were difficult to make in a prison where security was the prime concern. Yet in October 2013, the prison's budget was slashed and staff numbers drastically cut at the same time as established working practices were rejected in favour of new ways of working. 'It was,' said a senior management figure in the Prison Service, 'the most dramatic change in a hundred years.'

It was a recipe for disaster, and in my view it has been just that. The public don't hear in detail how prisoners are now being managed in what we would like to call a civilised 21st century society. But if animals were kept in such conditions I expect there would have already been a national uproar. It is difficult too for the public to fully appreciate the enormous strain that prison officers and governors have been under as they go about their duties.

In addition, two weeks after the regime was launched, when staff were still struggling with the new demands and prisoners were making threats of all kinds, plans were implemented to bring young offenders aged eighteen and upwards to Wormwood Scrubs, a prison that had until then catered for male adults of 21-plus. It was a desperate measure and came about because Feltham Prison for young offenders was in a perilous state.

Seasoned and dedicated men and women on the staff, some of whom have worked in prisons for nearly thirty years, told me that conditions had become so bad that for the first time in their working lives they feared for their safety.

This is not to ignore the need to make substantial cuts in the public sector as a result of the financial meltdown and that providing funds for prisons isn't a vote winner for any government, whatever its political persuasion. But I believe the cuts and reforms have reached a point where there are serious and valid concerns about the safety and welfare of both prisoners and staff that should no longer be concealed. My view was reinforced when in June 2014 Nick Hardwick, Chief Inspector of Prisons spoke on the BBC Radio 4's Today programme and gave an unexpectedly blunt warning about prison conditions. Hardwick, a man at pains to avoid controversy, said that the system was not coping and warned that, because of staff shortages, men were locked up together for 23 hours a day, causing 'huge tension.' He added that the problem had arisen because 'demands on the system have completely outstripped the resources available to them.' He also revealed that the numbers of men who had killed themselves in prison was at the highest level for almost ten years. That they were almost 80% up last year and in May 2014 alone 11 men killed themselves.

Justice Secretary Chris Grayling who was then interviewed on the news programme disagreed with Mr Hardwick's comments. He denied overcrowding and told Today there were currently 1,000 spare prison places and promised 2,000 new ones by April 2015. So that if some prisons were full and prisons had to double up in a cell it would only be a temporary measure. He added that the recent increase in prisoners could be linked to prosecutions for historic sex offences.

It was obvious to me that when the Chief Inspector of Prisons warns of the threat of serious disturbances it should be taken very seriously and proved without doubt that the problems affecting Wormwood Scrubs were replicated up and down the country. Certainly at the Scrubs the sweeping changes have brought about an increase in violence and self-harming. Officers have even referred to some prisons as 'warzones.' They have also significantly reduced prisoners' chances of rehabilitation. Instead, they have increased the likelihood of their reoffending, which is the opposite of what the Coalition says it wants to achieve. I believe it is in the public interest to bring out what is happening into the open. As one long-serving officer said to me: 'Prisoners are now being treated more appallingly than when I first started nearly thirty years ago.'

The Coalition, the National Offender Management System (NOMS) and a few prison governors are not being open about what has gone disastrously wrong. Instead they have adopted a no-matter-what optimistic positive front, referring to the difficulties as teething troubles, perhaps in the hope they will all go away or no one will find out the truth.

It's why I decided to write a portrait of Wormwood Scrubs to let the public know what has really been going on behind the prison's intimidating iron gates, how life inside has been allowed to deteriorate over the past decade and the effect of the drastic changes. I also know that the problems in Wormwood Scrubs are found in other prisons up and down the country.

The book represents my personal view and no one else's. I have been careful not to reveal the identities of prisoners or staff. Nor am I blaming any specific individuals and particularly not the hard-working officers and governors who overall do an extraordinary job. The incidents and views I describe are all true, but in some cases they have been subtly altered so they cannot be attributed to any one individual. I have also been careful not to write anything that could compromise the prison regime or its security. The book describes the prison as it was before the October 2013 changes and how badly it has been affected by them.

- - - - - - - -

I know the prison extremely well. Members of the IMB are volunteers, independent and unpaid. Their role is to monitor the day-to-day life of a prison and ensure that proper standards of care and decency are maintained. It derived its responsibilities from the Prison Act 1952 and no prison or detainee centre in the country is allowed to run without a monitoring board.

I decided to volunteer to be an independent monitor because I have always been fascinated by those trapped in life's underbelly. I am also one of those middle-class individuals who want to give something back to society but I didn't want to be a lady who lunched or a charity fund-raiser. I am not a do-gooder with idealistic views on how to change the world. My interest was based on curiosity centred on what people at the bottom of the human pile were really like. I became a magistrate for four years but there was not enough direct connection with those individuals who came before me, so I left. The initial IMB interview was surprisingly straightforward. It was followed by my first experience of dealing with the Ministry of Justice, as it took nearly a year for the security check to be done and my appointment to be confirmed. Later when I was Chair of the Board and interviewed potential members – there was a list of specific questions – I was surprised how hard it was in practice to convince the IMB governing body to turn anyone down even if they were obviously unsuitable. Six weeks of training came next. This consisted of one three-hour evening session a week for six weeks, plus extra day-time sessions given by members of the prison staff on various aspects of the prison, including security. I felt it was nowhere near enough. There followed a year-long probationary period when I shadowed various established members round different areas of the prison. I couldn't believe how much there was to learn, how difficult it was to know the right person to ask for information and how hard it was for someone like me with no sense of direction to find their way around. Once I had covered all the areas, it was up to me to decide when I was ready to take the big step and go round on my own.

Monitors have unrestricted access to the prison at any time and can talk to any prisoner out of sight and hearing of the staff if necessary. Monitors are meant to play an important role in dealing with problems inside the establishment. If prisoners have an issue that they have been unable to resolve through the usual internal channels, they can put in a confidential request to see a member of the IMB. Likewise, if something serious happens, for example a riot or a death in custody, representatives of the board are expected to attend and observe the way in which the situation is handled. Monitors do not have input into management decisions but should observe the day to day running of the prison and comment on the effects it has on prisoners.

- - - - - - - -

As well as being an independent monitor for nearly ten years I spent the last three years as the Board's Chair. I saw how three different Governors worked and the unending pressure they were under.

Being Chair was a fascinating but time-consuming experience. As well as being responsible for monitoring a quarter of the prison once a month – it needs four monitors per month to cover the whole prison – duties of the Chair included a monthly private meeting with the Governor to discuss concerns and get an update on what was happening in the prison. The Chair also ran a monthly board meeting, part of which the Governor attends, to report and discuss what we found during our visits round the prison. Included in the meeting was a training session on an aspect of prison life. A key responsibility of the Chair was to produce, with input from other members, an annual report on the state of the prison for the Justice Secretary. This was also released to the press. In recent years we highlighted increasingly serious concerns. These were passed on to the Justice Department and Prison Service. I was politely thanked for my time and trouble but in response to my latest report informed that what I and other independent monitors had seen with our own eyes and been told over and over again by prisoners and staff simply wasn't so. I believe the public has a right to know the true state of affairs at Wormwood Scrubs.

- - - - - - - -

Wormwood Scrubs, often known as the Scrubs, has an extraordinary history. The last report on the prison by Her Majesty's Inspectorate of Prisons in November 2011 began: 'Wormwood Scrubs is probably the most famous prison in the country, its image produced in countless dramas and documentaries.'

Its imposing entrance and gates have long been the prison of choice for many films and TV series. Its famous prisoners have included the spy George Blake, Charles Bronson, who has been called the most difficult prisoner in Britain, the actor Leslie Grantham, Pete Doherty, musician and close friend of Kate Moss, the Rolling Stone Keith Richard, the jockey Timmy Murphy, and John Stonehouse, the Labour MP and Minister who faked his own death. It was also seen as such a powerful symbol of the capital that in 1975 it was named on a bombers' target list among a pile of papers in a flat occupied by IRA terrorists, along with army establishments, the Queen's Gallery in Buckingham Palace and the British Museum. It is also visited regularly, although few stay for long, by senior politicians in the UK and dignitaries from all over the world.

The introduction to the Inspectorate report continued: 'Of course, the reality behind the image is much less glamorous than many TV programmes suggest.' In fact, there is nothing glamorous about Wormwood Scrubs, a B category local male prison. B category is for prisoners who are thought not to need the highest level of security but still pose a risk to the public. It is situated between three tough estates, White City, Westwood and East Acton.

According to the Ministry of Justice the budget for Wormwood Scrubs for 2012-2013 was just under £26 million at an approximate cost per prisoner of £35,584. The budget allocated to the Governor covers the major costs of running the prison but excludes most of the costs of outsourced services like education and healthcare.

Local prisons are officially defined as a prison where a person is detained before a trial or directly after a conviction. They are notoriously difficult to manage. Convicted prisoners rarely stay put longer than ten weeks before being moved to another jail. Remand prisoners, who are awaiting trail, often stay for much longer. The Scrubs also houses foreign nationals and detainees awaiting deportation, who can be held at the prison for more than two years. Each of the three groups has very different needs, and what works for one group often doesn't for the other two.

At one end of the spectrum of public opinion are those who believe that prisoners should be locked up and not allowed televisions or computer games in their cells and certainly shouldn't be allowed to vote. At the other end are those who believe that whatever their crime, the prisoners are the victims and they should be treated accordingly. It is of course far more complex than that. Prisoners are as different as any other group of individuals. They also represent so much that has gone wrong with our society and the effects of the ill-thought-out, short-term decisions of governing politicians of all parties.

This includes the breakdown of the family unit, children being brought up in care, the chronic lack of male role models, especially for teenage boys, girls who have no self-respect or moral grounding and often have babies because they need someone to love them and sometimes because it will guarantee them a council flat. Tragically, their interest in their babies can diminish as the child grows up. It is in prison that you see the shocking effect of the cynical closure of mental health hospitals under the failed 'care in the community' policy espoused by both major political parties. This has resulted in prisons holding severely mentally ill individuals who should not be there but who are unable to cope with the world or themselves and have nowhere else to go. They end up confined to prison, where they are monitored and medicated but not treated.

- - - - - - - -

Then there is the education system that has failed to teach so many disturbed and dysfunctional kids how to read and write, our materialistic way of life and fifteen-minutes of fame culture that makes people feel they have a right to that 42" television set, designer trainers, and the latest iPhone without working for it, and the easy access to pornography. Plus there are games and films that show graphic violence and desensitise those who make a habit of watching them. There is also the failure of the country's immigration policy that lets in many individuals who gravitate to an already crowded capital and who barely know more than how to claim benefits and enter an underworld of petty crime.

All these issues have been well aired in one form or another, but over time they have combined to create a twisted sub-culture of people who are largely doomed to stay in a subterranean world of their own. To stand on a busy prison wing or corridor when hundreds of such men are moving from one part of the jail to another is an extraordinary and unforgettable experience. So much criminality in one place reeks of malevolence and makes your heart race, however calm you try to appear – the more so if you are female.

Meanwhile, politicians and officials come up with wide-ranging proposals for change and seem to take little notice of those who work with prisoners and disapprove of their ideas. Instead they are told they have somehow got to make it work. Goalposts are moved seemingly at whim, there is a one-size-fits-all approach and procedures and practices are changed with astonishing frequency, making it ever more difficult for anyone to do a decent job. Sometimes just the names of policies are changed and very little else. Targets and box-ticking seem to take precedence over common sense.

The recent changes in working practices are undermining the crucial relationship between prison officer and inmate. Prisoners are locked in their cells for long periods, and while the government talks about rehabilitation there are often not enough staff to even unlock the cells so they can be taken to a training course. Addicts, rather than be weaned off drugs are indulged and leave the prison in almost the same state or sometimes worse than the one in which they arrive. It makes them even less likely to cope with the world outside. Meanwhile the number of prisoners continues to rise. According to official figures at the beginning of June 2014 there were 81,222 male prisoners in England and Wales. This compares to 42,000 males in jail in 1992.

The question independent monitors are supposed continually to ask themselves when they tour a prison is 'is it fair, decent and reasonable?' I don't think that what was happening in Wormwood Scrubs and, as officers regularly told me, in many other prisons round the country, is fair, decent or reasonable.

When new IMB members are appointed, they are told how valuable they are as the 'eyes and ears' of the Ministry of Justice. I have written this book because no one is listening.

CHAPTER ONE
A DAY IN THE LIFE

A chill wind is blowing as I unlock the outer and inner iron doors that lead into one of the wings of HMP Wormwood Scrubs prison in west London. I am on my rounds keeping an eye on what is going on. There is no prison officer with me. I have been given a set of keys and will walk about on my own.

It is mid-morning and 'association time', when prisoners are let out of their cells to mix with fellow inmates, play pool, get their hair cut by another inmate or make phone calls. The prison is not a predictable environment. The atmosphere in a wing can change in an instant. The majority of prisoners are both vulnerable and unpredictable. Many easily become violent, so when the cells are unlocked and the prisoners are out in the wing it's important to stay both alert and calm. I don't feel scared but I am always wary.

I am in the smallest of the four main wings which has space for 176 prisoners. I have only just signed in at the entrance when a pale thin prisoner rushes up to me. He has recognised my badge that shows I belong to the Independent Monitoring Board.

He tells me his name and stands far too close, but insists he needs to whisper important information in my ear. He looks to his right and left then confides he knows something secret and 'really bad' about how another prisoner has died in custody. I move away a little, not least because he smells as if he hasn't showered for a while. It's a common problem as the temperature in the wing is often far too hot.

He is wearing a cotton prison regulation pale turquoise T shirt and I notice he has long bloodied scars up both his arms, a sign of self-harming. He says he wants to tell the Prisons and Probation Ombudsman about what happened to the dead prisoner but fellow inmates have warned him that if he does he will put himself in danger. Instead he will tell me. But first he wants me to deal with another problem. He claims he is being poisoned by the staff who also spit in his food and put string and glue into whatever he eats.

It's unwise to take anything a prisoner tells you at face value and I merely nod to his accusations. Research shows that about 72% of sentenced male prisoners suffer from two or more mental disorders and it doesn't take many visits to Wormwood Scrubs to believe the same applies here.

I have not been trained to deal with men like him. All I remember is that the governor in charge of security made it clear that I should never go into any prisoner's cell, however much a prisoner wants to talk in private. The most seriously mentally ill inmates are kept in the health wing, known as H3, but the unit only has seventeen beds. The remainder are housed on a regular wing or the Segregation Unit, known as the Seg, and prison officers have to do their best to deal with them with the very minimum of training.

I manage to extricate myself from him after about thirty minutes of almost unintelligible conversation. He, like many prisoners, has problems expressing himself clearly and logically. Instead he rambles, changing the subject matter and the time sequence until I feel dizzy and confused. I have however taken some notes and promise to investigate. I first go to see the landing officer, a member of staff who has a small office on a wing landing and usually knows all about the prisoners on his watch.

Luckily he is at his desk and tells me that the prisoner I have spoken to should be in a mental health unit not in prison, that he is a heroin addict and that his self-harming is on the increase. He does, however, know nothing about the alleged suicide. I wonder if it is the prisoner who hanged himself with torn up strips of blanket that the senior governor told me about three weeks previously. I decide to check when I go back to the admin block.

I haven't moved far when another prison officer approaches me and asks me to see a prisoner whose cell is on a higher landing. The previous day he had smashed the toilet and sink in his cell and caused a significant flood. This behaviour is a recognised outlet for a prisoner's frustration and takes a regular toll on the prison budget. The officer is concerned that he seems very on edge.

The officer unlocks the cell and he comes out to talk to me. He tells me the prison officers and the governors have all got it in for him. That he had been told he could be released on licence but they have now withdrawn the offer and he has documents to prove it. It is common practice for prisoners to serve part of their sentence in the community as long as they adhere to certain rules and see their probation officer regularly. I originally thought that anyone released early would be only too pleased to keep to a few basic rules, but in practice countless numbers of prisoners do not, are re-arrested and come back to the prison to serve out their sentence in full.

The prisoner's attitude is not unusual. Paranoia is endemic amongst prisoners who believe that officers and governors 'have it in' for them. It is incorrect but occasionally an officer isn't as controlled as he should be when a particular prisoner has got on his nerves. It is something I watch out for carefully.

Officers cannot on a whim stop a prisoner being released on licence. This is up to the parole board and like everything else in prison, is controlled by a special procedure. I ask him if he still has the paperwork that withdraws his right to be released. He invites me into his cell, I suggest I wait where I am. He rushes inside and produces it triumphantly. I skim through the documents and see nothing negative. A thought enters my head and I tactfully ask him if he can read. He admits he can't but says one of his mates read the documents to him. I tell him that his mate was probably playing a practical joke as the document merely asks for basic information, including the address where he will be living once he is released, as this has to be approved by his probation officer. He looks at me in utter amazement. 'Oh Miss, really?' he asks. He then hangs his head. 'Miss, I can't write nice so I don't know how to fill in the form.'

I offer to help, read each paragraph out to him and take down the information he gives me. He is movingly grateful. The next time he sees me on the wing he waves and smiles. 'Thanks so much for that Miss. Made my day.' It was the simplest thing to do but in the confined world of the prison little things become magnified and supremely important. I wonder what chance someone so illiterate has coping with the world outside.

- - - - - - - -

Prisoners' attitude to me and other members of the Board varies hugely. Some are grateful that we can help sort out a whole range of problems for them, others dismiss us as useless, often because we don't tell them what they want to hear or decline to be used to run errands. Another prison officer approaches and asks for a private word. My role is focused on prisoners so I am a little reluctant to get involved. Not least because most prison officers are members of the Prison Officers Association and have a union to sort out their difficulties. But if a prison officer is out of sorts, his mood can affect the prisoners. So I follow him to talk at the end of the wing where it is quiet. He is white, young and pale skinned.

He explains that a group of black prisoners are making racist remarks about him and deliberately trying to wind him up. 'It's not fair Miss,' he complains. 'I have to watch myself when I talk to a non-white prisoner, but they are allowed to say what they like to me. It's really got me stressed.' It's a difficult issue and we talk for several minutes.

I suggest he speaks to his union representative and I will bring the problem up at my next meeting with the senior Governor. He and I have a private meeting once a month a few days before the Board's monthly meeting, to discuss concerns and issues. It's a valuable time and the perfect opportunity to mention any problems. The officer asks to remain anonymous. He is scared of retribution by a more senior officer.

I walk over to a green metal post box fixed to a wall of the wing. It's where prisoners post requests to the IMB for help when they have a problem. There are four forms inside with the details of the prisoner's name, his prison number and which cell he occupies. Their requests are called applications, are confidential and not seen by staff. One prisoner has filled the whole form vertically and horizontally with capital letters. One line reads 'DEAL WITH THIS URGENCY AS TO MY RIGHTS AND PROTOCOL.' I make a note, then put it aside.

The first prisoner I visit is on the fourth floor. I climb three metal staircases that are thick with grime. Prisoners are given jobs to keep the wing clean but for some reason, the stairs are regularly neglected. I walk the length of the wing to check that the prisoner is in fact in the cell number that is on the sheet. I open the latch in the door and call his name. A Chinese man jumps up from the narrow single bed and identifies himself. I leave him to walk back along the length of the wing to find the landing officer to ask if he is safe and can come out of his cell and speak to me. He says he's no problem and we walk back together so he can unlock his door. I have keys to every area in the prison but not to individual cells.

The Chinese prisoner asks me to help him get £2,000 and his passport that he claims were taken from him in a police station in 2007. It's now 2010 and I ask if he has written proof that this has happened. He doesn't, but knows they took it. I also ask why he has waited so long to report the matter. He replies he was homeless until he arrived in the prison nearly three weeks ago.

I wonder how a homeless person can accumulate such a large sum and unusually ask why he is in prison. Money laundering he says. Fortunately I have a solid reason why I can't even begin to investigate and tell him that my role is to help with issues that occur in the prison, not outside. I suggest he speaks to his lawyer. He tells me the lawyer says it is not her job. I tell him it is definitely not mine. He doesn't seem surprised.

The third prisoner is obviously in his fifties and extremely polite. He explains he wanted to send his wife some money that the prison's accounts department took £150 out of his personal account and he arranged for the cash to be sent by recorded delivery to his home.

Although he has had confirmation that the money was removed from his account, the recorded delivery document was not stamped and the letter has not arrived at its destination. The incident happened over three months ago and in the meantime he has spoken to the wing governor and a host of other members of staff, which is much more difficult than it sounds. They have admitted the fault seems to be with the prison but no one has authorised that the money should be put back in his account. It is just the sort of issue I can help sort out once I am back in the admin building.

I then take a deep breath and go to find the prisoner who has written in capitals all over his form. 'I am waiting for two days,' he starts aggressively. 'Why you so late?' I try to explain that IMB members are not employed by the prison, that we are volunteers and we don't visit each wing every day. He is Polish and so cross with my response that he decides he doesn't want to speak to me. 'You no good,' he says with a flourish and slams the door of his cell. I am quietly relieved.

It is now 11.30am and lunch is being served. There are five choices of dish, including halal and vegetarian, plus rice, boiled potatoes, boiled carrots and piles of sliced bread. I move to the server and decide to wait to see how the prisoner who accused officers of poisoning his food, fares. There is a long queue of prisoners waiting for their unappetising looking meal, but eventually he gets to the front. He points to a specific meat pie on a hotplate of about ten and it is transferred to his plate. He declines all vegetables and sets off to return to his cell. No one tries to give him a different pie, nor could a member of staff have been able to foresee when he would reach the server and keep a doctored pie ready for him.

I sign out of the wing locking the inner and outer wing doors behind me. It is a windy day and litter is blowing around freely. The litter is a real health hazard and I complain about it regularly. The senior Governor recently mentioned he may get some feral cats to help keep the rats and mice at bay. He hasn't yet investigated the matter as he is worried about the dogs who regularly go round the prison sniffing for drugs. He is concerned about what might happen if the feral cats attack them, or indeed an inmate.

I stop off at the line of workshops where some prisoners spend part of the day. Very few prisoners have what one might call a work ethic and often use the time to loll about chatting. It's hard to blame them as the work is often dull and pointless. They do however earn a little while they are there, which means they can buy tobacco, toiletries or extra food to supplement what is supplied by the prison.

My next stop is the Healthcare Unit. It takes several minutes to walk there as I have to unlock and re-lock at least eight double iron doors as I pass through the prison. I feel most on edge in the health wing that houses physically and mentally ill prisoners, partly because of the unpredictability of some of the prisoners and partly because I don't want to catch anything. They do not have hand-wash gel at the entrance.

I sign in and ask the officer in charge for an update on the prisoners. She tells me about a prisoner on suicide watch. One member of staff is sitting outside his cell eyes fixed on him except for the few moments when she makes notes in a book. The cell door is wide open but an iron gate ensures the staff member's safety and a clear view. The prisoner is lying on his side under a thin blanket on his bed. I ask him if he is okay but he doesn't reply.

I am told he has a temperature of 39 degrees and has swine flu, but won't take his medication. I instinctively ask for the date he allowed the saliva swabs to be taken, partly because it shows a re-assuring willingness on his part to co-operate. A prison nurse says he didn't allow it, but they have been instructed by someone on high that every prisoner who has a high temperature should be put down as having swine flu. It is January 2010 and a few months later the Ministry of Health state that almost half of the population has caught swine flu during the latest pandemic. It confirms my belief that you should never trust statistics.

- - - - - - - -

My next stop is the Segregation Unit, known as the Seg. This is the prison within the prison. It houses up to eighteen vulnerable or mentally ill prisoners who are prone to being violent, very difficult prisoners and those who need to be kept safe for their own protection. Prisoners have their own code of what crimes are okay and those that are not. They often take justice into their own hands and paedophiles, for example, are often attacked. Also in the Seg are prisoners who have been found with an illegal object like a mobile phone or drugs and those who have been in a fight with either prisoners or staff.

Spending virtually all day alone with their thoughts, is for some the worst of all punishments. The staff who are specially trained and chosen with care do a valiant job coping with unpredictable, often violent behaviour. It is a serious and potentially dangerous place. One prisoner, an Irish traveller, has been constantly pressing the bell in his cell for over five minutes. It is loud and there for emergencies but is a standard way to get an officer's attention. He had also started banging on his cell door.

Another prisoner screams obscenities from inside his cell to tell him to stop. Apparently he has kept the unit up most of the previous night and everyone is fed up with him. Two officers accompany me to his cell. 'I can't stand it here,' he wails when the door is open. 'I am going mad. I can't be on my own. I feel suicidal.'

Threatening suicide is often little more than a way of getting attention, but works because officers can't risk ignoring it. The prisoner wants a television, but that is not allowed in the Seg. I suggest a radio, only to discover that so many have been deliberately smashed by prisoners that the prison is waiting for a new delivery.

At 12.30pm the prison goes into 'shut down.' All prisoners are locked in their cells and staff reduced to an absolute minimum so that officers can have a lunch break. It's not fair to delay the staff so I go back to the admin block and sort out the problem of the missing cash. It seems the prisoner who complained that his £150 hasn't left the prison is absolutely right. The registered letter didn't go out, but nor had authority been given for the £150 to be put back in the prisoner's account. The prison is sometimes slow when it comes to financial compensation, but things traditionally start to move once the IMB gets involved.

Today will be a long day as I have been asked to take a delegation of Russians round Wormwood Scrubs. I am told that President Putin is interested in the British system of independent monitoring and is considering using something similar for Russian prisons. It seems hard to believe, but welcome if it's true. A delegation of nine including a judge, prison governor and human rights activists plus an interpreter have asked to see Wormwood Scrubs and are due this afternoon. It is understandably difficult to get into a prison. A mountain of documents have been processed in advance and all members of the delegation have been told to bring their passports and other forms of identification.

Six of them arrive an hour late much to the exasperation of the individual involved in inter-prison cooperation who has collected them from the centre of town. The interpreter didn't fly over to keep the costs down. I go over to the gatehouse entrance and find a chaotic scene. One of the group has brought several bottles of vodka which he doesn't want to hand over. I struggle to make myself understood using simple English and exaggerated gestures that it is illegal to take alcohol into a prison. They all laugh at my hand movements but obviously disagree. A similar argument takes place over their cameras and mobile phones both of which are also forbidden in a jail. It is not a negotiable position but it takes almost an hour before they give in, the administration is done and they are finally let into the prison.

I cut my planned programme in half as there now won't be time to do very much. They don't seem to mind and mention 'shopping' and 'Oxford Street'. They are keen to go to a wing, to see the food the prisoners eat and visit the Segregation Unit. They also ask where I keep my gun. I explain with a shake of the head and using my fingers to make a passable gun shape that I don't have one. They are astonished. Once we reach a wing I explain in the same way that prison officers don't have guns either. They can't believe it. They ask if there are any Russians in the wing. I have no idea and try to spot an officer who can help.

It is never easy taking a group round a prison. I feel responsible for their safety and ask them by means of several gestures not to wander off on their own, especially as many prisoners are in the communal area. But while I am trying to explain some of the notices on the walls that highlight prisoners' rights, the wing timetable and the help available for drug addicts, a few wander off and peer into some open cells. I rush after them. Prisoners will take none too kindly to someone looking at or touching their things.

I suggest we move on and offer a trip to the kitchen where the prisoners' third meal of the day is being prepared. I explain that prisoners have a choice of what they want to eat and the group shake their heads in disbelief and talk excitedly together. 'Good, good' they marvel at the food. I raise my eyebrows in disbelief. 'In Russia, no, no, no' one says, which I assume means it is nothing like this in Russian prisons.

The prison partly closes down at 5.30pm when the day shift officers go off duty and I gently usher the group back to the entrance. They collect their cameras, phones and vodka then triumphantly hand me a Russian tie clip, army hat and a bottle of vodka to thank me for my time. I thank them profusely. Sometimes I wonder why I spend so much time to try to ensure that prisoners are treated humanely and with decency as it is often frustrating and always incredibly sad, but today I leave with a smile.

CHAPTER TWO
WELCOME TO THE SCRUBS

N ew prisoners arrive at Wormwood Scrubs from police stations or local courts in west London, north west London, and parts of central London. In March 2011 Serco was given a £297 million seven-year contract – the most expensive ever within the Ministry of Justice – to ferry prisoners to and from these courts and between prisons in London and East Anglia.

The outsourced Prisoner Escort and Custody Services (PECS) began operating in August, six months later. It was chaos. Serco was required to transport about 900 prisoners a day of whom about 40-60 plus were driven to and from Wormwood Scrubs. Serco didn't have enough vans in operation and those that were available didn't get out on the road early enough. It meant that prisoners arrived in court late and cases often had to be held up or postponed.

Prisoners who were on time for their cases to be heard often then had to wait several hours in court cells for Serco staff to pick them up and take them back to prison. Once collected, they could spend hours being driven round while other prisoners in the vans were dropped off. As a result, prisoners destined for Wormwood Scrubs often arrived so late that they were locked out for the night. After 9pm the prison operates with minimum staff and the main gate is closed. Late prisoners had to be taken to a police station to be housed in their cells. The police were not keen to take them in partly because they didn't know if they had mental health issues or were suicidal.

Serco soon admitted that 'things were not going according to plan' that they were not 'operating as we want to operate' and that they had wanted a 'seamless transfer'. They also claimed it was not entirely their fault, stating that they had been told by the Ministry of Justice that they would have an eight-month 'mobilisation' plan. Instead the Ministry, apparently rather late in the day, decided it wanted Serco to commence operations after six months. It was unfortunate that Serco chose to combine the introduction of their escort service with setting up a new IT system. This went live the day before the escort contract started but then crashed on the first day of operation. As a result vans went to the wrong place, or drivers got lost so staff were not in the right court at the right time. The company simultaneously changed its management structure and moved the control room from Banbury in Oxfordshire to Gloucester. To make matters worse, all this coincided with the sudden spike of prisoners as a result of the London riots in the summer of 2011, which in fairness Serco couldn't have been prepared for.

Serco had a total of 184 vans, of which about 27 were expected to be out of action at any one time due to refurbishment. The company had 28 days advance warning on how many prisoners they had to pick up from crown courts but only heard at 4am of the day in question the number they had to transport from magistrates' courts. There was no provision in the vans for seatbelts and very few had toilets. There was, however, an emergency 'toilet' for female prisoners: it was described to me as being as a 'type of potty that has a type of cat litter'. It's hard to imagine how degrading this must be.

Instead prisoners were allowed a 'comfort break' every two and a half hours. They could not be taken to a public toilet for security reasons. Instead, the van had to stop at a prison, court or police station. It was a complex procedure to log each prisoner in and out so the stop-over could be very time-consuming. Women and men were often transported together which could be risky if a male prisoner had committed a sexual offence or if some of them (of either sex) were violent.

Many of the vehicles were not large enough to take the prisoners' property. On many occasions the vans had a full complement of prisoners and no room for their possessions. It was as time-consuming as it was difficult to establish whether these possessions had gone missing while in the hands of Serco or at the prison. The vans had drinking water but no food. Prisoners who had spent hours waiting in a court cell and subsequently been driven around various prisons often arrived at the Scrubs during the evening, unfed and tense.

As a result I, as Chair of the Independent Monitoring Board at Wormwood Scrubs, invited representatives of Serco to address us at our October 2011 Board meeting. I also invited the monitoring boards of Pentonville, Wandsworth and Brixton prisons to join us as they had also expressed concerns about the transportation of prisoners. Three senior representatives of Serco arrived. I had previously collated the key questions and issues the various boards were concerned about and sent them through three weeks in advance so the representatives could hopefully be specific in their answers. Instead it was an extraordinary exercise in evasion and lack of transparency.

In the IMB's 2012 report for the Justice Secretary, which I wrote from material gathered by my fellow Board members, we heavily criticised Serco for its service between the courts and the prison. The report detailed the cancellations, the over-crowding of vehicles, the lack of food and the on-board 'potty.'

Nor did Serco handle inter-prison transfers efficiently. Wormwood Scrubs, in common with other prisons, was often not informed when a transfer would not take place. It could even be cancelled at the last minute. This meant that those prisoners who were on the transfer list were kept in 'holding rooms' in the Reception area, along with their property, from 9am waiting for the van, only to be returned to their cells in the afternoon. It was a tense time for prisoners and made unnecessary work for staff.

There were also general slip-ups. One prisoner was taken to court on time but once the van arrived Serco staff realised they did not have the keys to unlock the vehicle to let him out. His hearing had to be postponed. Other prisoners were delivered to the wrong court. New prisoners who arrived at the jail were usually far too late for the regular evening prison meal, which was served at 4.30pm, but subsequently staff managed to organise some food for them. Prisoners complained about how they had been treated. One grievance was that Serco staff mentioned their crimes in front of the others in the van. The chaos affected both staff and prisoners.

Staff in Reception and the First Night Centre, a small wing for first-timers, ended their shift at 9pm. On many occasions prisoners hadn't even been delivered by then. Once they arrived, they could not be dealt with quickly. Health and safety checks had to be completed, not least to ensure that vulnerable or dangerous prisoners were identified. The ferrying service improved over time but the timing remained unreliable. In mid-2013 Serco was found to have the worst delivery rate for the number of Crown Court trials being stopped and re-started because the company had failed to produce the defendant. At the same time Justice Secretary Chris Grayling asked the Serious Fraud Office to investigate allegations that Serco had overcharged the government 'tens of millions of pounds' for tagging people who were dead, in prison or had left the country. Serco has also been under investigation for allegedly overcharging for ferrying prisoners to courts. Serco subsequently agreed to repay all past profits, believed to be about £68.5m plus VAT, made on the PECS contract and to forgo any future profits. It also withdrew its bid to be lead providers in the privatisation of the probation service.

When the vans finally arrived they would drive through the prison's famous huge Victorian iron gates. The relevant paperwork would be checked and the prisoners taken to Reception. It is the responsibility of the Reception unit to process prisoners in and out of the jail. They were very busy first thing in the morning ensuring prisoners were ready to be taken to court, and that those who were being transferred, discharged, sent to immigration centres, or had hospital appointments were properly dealt with. The unit would be very busy again in the late afternoon and evening when prisoners arrived from court or as transfers. The majority arrived after 5pm. On average, Reception processed several hundreds of men in and out of the jail each week. This high turnover created many challenges. It was difficult to manage all the prisons who had complex health issues but important that major problems were identified early. Sometimes forty prisoners could arrive at once. A prison officer remarked 'it resulted in prisoners being treated as if they were cattle in a market.'

-- -- -- -- --

The routine was that newly-arrived prisoners approached the reception desk one at a time where they were first asked basic questions including their name, date of birth and if they had been in prison before. I listened to this countless time and always wondered how, without pausing or changing the tone of his voice, the officer in charge would then ask the prisoner whether he wanted to cut or kill himself. It was an important question but not easy to answer with a 'yes' or 'no' in public.

Close to the reception desk was a sign in capital letters that read: WORMWOOD SCRUBS IS COMMITTED TO PROVIDING A SECURE SAFE AND CARING ENVIRONMENT WHERE PRISONERS AND STAFF CAN LIVE AND WORK TOGETHER WITHOUT FEAR OF VIOLENCE THREAT OR ABUSE. VIOLENCE IN ANY FORM WILL NOT BE ACCEPTED AND WILL BE CHALLENGED WHEN AND WHEREVER IT OCCURS.

I never saw any prisoner stop to read it. Fingerprints and photographs were also taken and men who had never been in prison before were given a prison number. They were also led to a room where they were strip-searched and their possessions taken to the property store.

Once the necessary questions were completed, prisoners sat in small groups in bare holding rooms, sometimes for up to three or four hours. Some of them looked shell-shocked, most were subdued and placid. Occasionally there was violence. One prisoner kept walking up and down in the Reception area and wouldn't answer any of the staff's questions. He then took off all his clothes. He was obviously very unwell but it needed six officers to convey him out of the Reception area, along a corridor, up some stairs and into a cell in the healthcare unit. Another who thought he was Elvis Presley became very volatile but it took 48 hours before there was space to move him to the healthcare wing. A third screamed all night that his cell was on fire. Officers often found it disturbing to deal with the number of mentally-ill prisoners who arrived. One commented. 'They have so many issues and we are not trained to do all the stuff necessary. Those who come here for the first time are not properly looked after, in my view.'

The large number of prisoners being processed each day also meant that the information collected at Reception was confined to their immediate needs and only provided essential information for the prison.

Procedures included a urine test to find out if a prisoner was on drugs and a risk assessment to ascertain whether they could share a cell with another inmate. Once the paperwork and these initial checks were completed, a few prisoners at a time were then taken to the First Night Centre, a small unit, up several flights of stairs, where a nurse and doctor would examine them. Staff shortages often meant prisoners had to wait several hours before someone was free to accompany them to the First Night Centre. Although officers did their best, when numbers were high they would sadly state it was 'not good enough.'

In the summer of 2011 an acute shortage of nurses meant that when the day staff left and the night staff came in at 10pm there could be as many as twenty prisoners still waiting to be screened and only one nurse around to handle the process. The situation was made worse when the nurse was called away to an emergency in another wing. As a result the screenings could sometimes take until 2am to be completed. The staff blamed a change in shift patterns but the same situation existed in the early part of 2014.

Most officers from the First Night Centre understood how traumatic it could be for someone to find himself behind bars in an alien environment. One told me that the 'loud prisoners are usually going to be OK. It's the quiet ones that need to be watched. Overall it is always the middle-class prisoner who is most traumatised. The majority have family who have been inside even if they haven't.' It was proof of how crime can run in families.

The wing had several dormitory rooms, which could be some comfort for prisoners who did not want to be alone. There were also two 'safe cells' for potentially dangerous or vulnerable prisoners. These had CCTV and were designed not to contain anything that could be used with a ligature. One prisoner confessed to me that he was terrified during his first night in jail. 'The worst thing was the noise,' he said. 'I lay in bed thinking that whoever was shouting might come and kill me.'

The greatest risk of suicide or self-harm was in the first seven days of a newly-arrived prisoner, particularly if he didn't speak English. Sometimes another prisoner was used as an interpreter rather than bringing in a professional. This was cheaper and quicker but ran the risk that the new prisoner did not want to tell another prisoner intimate details about himself and didn't disclose important information.

Although officers took great care to observe newcomers as they settled in, fear and shame can be a lethal combination and over the years there were several suicide attempts in the unit, some of which were sadly successful. In January 2008 a remand prisoner who spoke Tamil and virtually no English, was in the prison for only two days before he was found hanged in his communal cell at 4.24am by one of his cellmates who had woken to go to the toilet. A ligature around his neck was attached to the window bars. The staff had made strenuous efforts to put him at his ease when he arrived. They had found another Tamil-speaking prisoner to talk to him and by chance the prison doctor on duty also spoke Tamil and agreed to act as interpreter.

It was standard practice to offer a new prisoner who smoked a smoker's pack, which consisted of 12.5g of tobacco, cigarette papers and a lighter. Non-smokers could have instead a pack containing sweets, biscuits and squash. Both packs cost about £3.50, an amount that would later be deducted from the prison account that each prisoner set up to pay for extras. They were also allowed a personal phone call. A sign by the phone left prisoners with no doubt about where they were. It read: 'Be advised up to 50% of social calls are monitored.' One remand prisoner from Iraq demanded via a translator an unlimited time to make a call home. He said no one in his family knew that he had come to London and that his wife was having both a brain and heart operation. He was allowed a call but it had to be relatively brief. In addition, prisoners were given their breakfast pack before going to bed. This included a small pack of cereal, sugar, teabags and whitener.

- - - - - - - -

Early the following morning new prisoners would start the induction process to learn how the prison operated, what they were entitled to, what they could and couldn't do and how various organisations, including the independent monitors, could help them.

They then used to be taken to an induction wing but since October 2013 new prisoners have instead been spread around different wings. During the morning they would get their own telephone Personal Identification Number (PIN). In order to make calls they had to credit their prison account with money and register the phone numbers. They would also have talks from a chaplain, drug services and organisations such as the Citizens Advice Bureau

(CAB) and St Mungo's, which offered housing advice. In addition they would learn about the education department, workshops, gym and library.

Every individual was given prison policy statements, stating that the prison was 'committed, through care and understanding, to provide a safe, humane and positive environment for prisoners'; that it took a 'zero-tolerance ' approach to bullying, and that prisoners should tell staff, in confidence, if this happened to them; that the prison did not tolerate 'any form of harassment or unfair discrimination on the grounds of gender, marital status, race, colour, nationality, ethnic or national origin, disability, religion, sexual orientation, age or any other irrelevant factor', and that incidents should be reported by using a Racial Incident Reporting Form, that they would be taken seriously; and that the prison was 'dedicated to the prevention of discriminatory practices towards disabled people,' and that they should tell staff of any disabilities they had.

In spite of all these assurances, life on the wings would inevitably be intimidating, confusing, noisy and profoundly frustrating. Prisoners complained about everything and anything. Some complaints were justified, others less so. The process of complaining involved filling in a special form with details of what they felt was wrong. The form then went to one of the governors to investigate. If a prisoner didn't get a reply in an allotted timescale or still felt aggrieved he could appeal within the prison or contact the Prisons and Probation Ombudsman. He could also contact a monitor, such as myself.

Complaints were supposed to be taken seriously by prison staff. In practice this was not always so. The replies often addressed procedure rather than the actual concern. Nor were they clearly signed by the relevant governor as they should have been. Having struggled with endless numbers of unreadable scrawled signatures we requested over and over again that governors write their names in capitals under their signature so monitors would know who to approach on behalf of the prisoner when there were further issues. A senior governor agreed when I showed him specific evasive replies accompanied by a scrawl that it wasn't good enough, but things only improved for a short time before the capital letters disappeared and we were left with illegible signatures again. It was a small thing but made me uneasy. Perhaps whoever was dealing with the complaint was short of time, had more pressing priorities, or genuinely thought he was being helpful, but it certainly didn't give that impression.

Common complaints included not being let out for exercise on a particular day, being unfairly dismissed from a job within the prison, non-payment of wages, alleged victimisation by a member of staff, inadequate treatment by the prison's medical team, and what many referred to as 'abuse of process.'

A monitor's role was to help prisoners with matters both big and small that weren't 'fair or reasonable.' We were not there to be dogsbodies. One Irish traveller – travellers counted for about one in ten of the prisoners – demanded we provided him with some Irish music to help him relax.

It's why there was space on the IMB application forms for prisoners to write down what efforts they had made to sort out the issue for themselves.

One prisoner took exception to this. In the space left for him to explain what he had done about his problem, he wrote: 'Nothing, I can't be expected to do everything.' He received a brisk reply that stated politely that indeed he wasn't expected to do 'everything', but he needed to show he had done 'something.'

Another prisoner presented me with a list of twelve issues he wanted dealt with. These included that prisoners were planning to kill him, that officers let them abuse him, that his mail was not posted, he was not allowed to make phone calls, hadn't been able to change his clothes for weeks, and had been refused both a pillow and a towel. A quick conversation with a senior officer revealed that the prisoner had mental health issues and that the reason he didn't have a pillow or towel was because he kept refusing them. I asked for someone from healthcare to come and see him.

Because there was so little to occupy a prisoner's mind small things understandably took on huge significance. Prisoners obsessed about detail that wouldn't bother a busy or indeed a free person. It could be, for example, that a letter from home had got stuck in the postroom for a day or getting one sausage rather than two for lunch. Monitors were told to take these small issues seriously and an essential question for every applicant at the initial interview was to ask how they would cope with something that seemed minor to them but was important to a prisoner.

— — — — — — — —

The act of writing and explaining a problem wasn't easy even for English-speaking prisoners and the desperately low standard of literacy, sentence structure and spelling was an eye-opener. For example there were applications with the word 'due' spelt 'jue', 'pregnant' spelt 'pregnents', and 'did not receive' was written as 'dashk risive'. It took a while to work out that a prisoner who said he wanted to speak to me for 'converdenece reason' actually meant 'in confidence.' It was considerably more difficult for those whose mother tongue was not English to explain what help they needed but the more active usually found someone who could translate what they wanted to say.

Some applications were desperately sad. One prisoner asked to see me because he 'feels helpless.' He wrote: 'I just want to get out of my cell and do some work or get educated. Thank you.' Another was touching in his determination not to commit more crime, but like many was perhaps voicing his hopes over experience.

'My children are in care and my life is a mess. I really want to sort my life out and I have begun to study law, but finding somewhere to live is really hard. I want to sort out my life but I don't want to be on the dole. I hate spongers. I love working. Do you think I could be a shop assistant? I am too old' – he was 48 – 'to go to prison any more and I'm not making millions of pounds robbing people.'

One was jauntily defiant. 'It is disgusting the way we are treated in here. I will speak to my MP on release and contact the press.' And 'the officers and governors in this prison are not doing there (sic) job properly. They breach human rights law you're a slave.'

Just talking to a prisoner could be a salutary experience. Many prisoners, perhaps from dysfunctional families who rarely talked together, had no idea how to relate an incident in a simple, clear manner or talk in a chronological way. One man became increasingly agitated as he tried to explain an issue to me as I couldn't grasp the thread of what he was trying to say.

At one point I asked how being left on a bus fitted in with a judge allegedly giving him the wrong release date. He said it had no connection but that he was trying to tell me about something that happened when he was ten when he was talking about the court case. He had muddled everything up. I suggested we split what he wanted to say into different parts so that I could discuss each one in turn. It took a while because he kept going off on irrelevant tracks without any explanation. When we'd finally finished, I relayed four separate issues back to him that I thought were causing problems. I explained I could help him with two, but that the other two were prison policy and impossible to change. He looked at me in amazement then gratitude and said he was so pleased he'd been to express himself so clearly. Prisoners need and want to be listened to but few members of staff have the time, so it is important that monitors are patient.

The requests for help varied enormously. Some ignored what a prison was basically for and instead had the attitude that it was almost like a health spa. One prisoner wrote: 'I have come into prison to have my back and teeth sorted but all that's happened is that I've gone on a waiting list.'

Another wrote: 'I have asked for a radio every day for the last three days I still haven't got it.' There are only so many radios, televisions and kettles in the prison. Many are smashed in anger and prisoners have to wait until the next scheduled delivery arrives. I could find out delivery dates but not hurry them up.

Some issues proved impossible to solve. One prisoner stated he had given an envelope containing a cheque for £200 to an officer and wanted reassurance that the amount had gone on his account. I discovered that a cheque had been handed in to the finance department by Reception but was returned to the prisoner as he was not allowed to hold so much money in his account. The prisoner insisted he had put it in an addressed envelope and asked an officer to post it for him.

All post must pass through the mail office to be checked so any member of staff who had posted it would have committed a serious offence. The prisoner didn't remember the officer's name but was concerned that his mother hadn't received the cheque. I asked several officers if they knew anything about this matter but none did.

It was always unpredictable how a day in the prison might go, and all too often it was difficult to achieve anything. Luckily there were also good days. It was particularly gratifying when a prisoner I had tried to encourage to write something about himself to take his mind off his troubles came up to me as I was walking through his wing. He said. 'Thank you for saying I should write about my life. It was like lancing a boil and has been the one thing that has kept me going.'

I would be asked on a regular basis to see a prisoner whose request to attend the funeral of a family member wasn't going through smoothly. This was always tricky as the request could have been a ruse to escape. It was also demanding on staff as, depending on the nature of the prisoner's crime, one, two or three officers would be needed to accompany him. It was a particular problem if the wing was short-staffed.

On the other hand the prison was sympathetic, at least in theory, to the humanitarian aspect of a prisoner who had lost a parent, sibling or child, and usually allowed them to attend the funeral. Grandparents, uncles and aunts were, on the other hand, considered to be outside the intimate family circle and not a priority. Prisoners disagreed and some would weep when they heard they might not be able to 'show respect'. There was no obvious way to judge whether they were crocodile or genuine tears.

The final decision was left to the Security Department. Sometimes the prisoner didn't know if he had permission to go until the last minute, and when the request was turned down, no reason beyond the fact that it was a security issue was given. On one occasion the prisoner had collected his suit from the property store and was ready to leave for his uncle's funeral when staff were told he wouldn't be allowed out. The wing staff asked for a member of the chaplain's team to go along to break the news; as I was in the wing at the time an officer asked if I too could talk to the prisoner once the chaplain had gone.

He was sad and angry in about equal measure, saying over and over again that it hadn't been fair to tell him so late and that his uncle was very important to him as he had virtually brought him up. I managed to get him permission to make a phone call to a member of his family. I also suggested that although he couldn't go to the funeral, there might not be the same objection to him quietly visiting the grave in the near future on his own, and that he should put in a request to this effect.

While some prisoners kept their crime to themselves, others were quite up front. 'I am here because they think I was helping a multimillionaire drug dealer but I was only very small part of the operation,' one told me. 'I am polite and respectful. I have just finished twenty years inside on a murder charge and now I am back because they say I have taken steps to kill someone else.' I had no idea whether to believe him.

———————

Running a safe, secure and fair wing depended on staff and prisoners working together and there was a carrot and stick approach to encourage prisoners to behave. Prisoners were divided into three categories, Basic, Standard and Enhanced, each with its own set of privileges. A fourth category, Entry, was added in November 2013 for all new prisoners. An Incentives and Earned Privileges (IEP) scheme was announced in April 2013 and took effect in November 2013. Among other things it announced a fourth category, Entry, for new prisoners. Prisoners who didn't behave were put down a grade and had privileges taken away from them, while those who did conform to the regime went up a level and got more.

The operating system was complicated and bureaucratic but basically a higher-graded convicted prisoner could have more visits, get a better rate of the very low pay for any work he did, be allowed to use more of his own private cash and spend more time out of his cell. Higher-graded prisoners could also wear their own clothes, and even buy hair-clippers and a CD player via mail order. No electrical devices with a USB point were allowed as they could be used to charge a mobile. Enhanced prisoners were allowed a TV in their cell. The amount of personal cash a convicted prisoner could spend on toiletries and food varied from £4 a week to £25. Prisoners were put on Basic for several reasons including 'unreasonable behaviour', disobeying prison rules, intimidating prisoners and working to an unacceptable standard. They hated being on Basic and often wrote to the monitors to say how unfair it was.

Although the categories were set up to work as an incentive, prisoners often alleged that several officers used them as a threat. Often the complaint said more about the prisoner, than any officer. One prisoner who had been downgraded for bad behaviour was told he would no longer be allowed to have a television. 'It's not fair that if I damage a TV they don't give me another one,' he insisted. I told him an officer had reported that he had used the television to hide a mobile. 'So what?' he replied, 'everyone has mobiles.'

Remand prisoners amounted to about 45% of the prisoners. They had different privileges and could wear their own clothes. Convicted prisoners, largely wore the prison-issue tracksuits, but could wear their own underpants and socks. They were only allowed one kit change and one fresh sheet and blanket per week.

Many new prisoners didn't realise they couldn't have clean kit every day. They complained that they were being victimised by officers who were deliberately making them wear dirty clothes 'for days at a time'. I don't know how much it helped to learn that it was the same for everyone. All clothes and bed linen issued by the prison had to be washed in the prison laundry, well away from the wing. While all the prisoner's own clothes had to be washed in the wing. There were, however, only a couple of washing machines to each wing, and as they could only be used when the men were allowed out of their cells, it was an on-going problem to get things clean.

It was equally difficult for inmates to keep themselves clean. Officially they were only entitled to one shower a week, but senior officers on the wings often allowed them to have more. When a prisoner wanted to give a good impression at his forthcoming trial, an officer would usually do his best to help. 'I have a five-week trial starting in the next few weeks,' one offender said. 'I want a shower every day so I arrive clean but the officers have said it is difficult to organise that early in the morning. I have told my lawyer that it is my human right to be clean.' I spoke to an officer who agreed that despite being busy getting prisoners ready to go to court first thing in the morning, he would do his best to allow him to have a shower either in the morning or evening each day.

This same prisoner complained about being unable to clean his cell. 'The floor is filthy. I've asked every single day for ten days for the right equipment to clean it but I haven't been given what I need.' There was a limited supply of cleaning materials and buckets on a wing but I managed to sort that out too. Prisoners react to life in their cell much like kids do at boarding school. Some make their bed immaculately, stick pictures on the wall and store a range of food on the window-sill. I was once surprised to see a practising Muslim, who had a substantial beard and wore a skull cap, with crude photographs of Western women on the wall of his single cell. 'What are you looking at?' he demanded when he saw my eyes stray briefly to the areas of exposed flesh. 'You are supposed to be helping me. Concentrate.' Others showed no interest in their cells, which often looked like a rubbish dump.

Small prisoners had a tough time in prison. This was not only because in the macho world of male prisons they were easily bullied, but because they also faced the humiliation of wearing over-long prison-issue tracksuit bottoms that trailed on the ground. One small prisoner nearly fell over his trousers as he rushed to catch me as I walked through a wing. He asked for help. 'I can't read or write,' he began, 'so I couldn't put one of those forms in the box for you. But I am beside myself. I've worn this same tracksuit for three weeks now. I fall over and stink and they won't give me anything clean because they say they haven't got my size.' I thought he might be exaggerating. He wasn't. He had worn the same clothes for weeks on end.

Nor was he a quiet prisoner who preferred not to make a fuss. In the three weeks he had been at the Scrubs he had made wild allegations about several officers, complained about not having a job, the 'awful' food and his cellmate. An officer said that he managed to bring out the worst in people. I could see he could be irritating but he was justified in his complaints about his clothes. Special sizes had to be ordered, but no one had done so for him. I asked for kit his size to be organised and some clean clothes to be given to him while he was waiting. When I saw him a couple of weeks later he was wearing tracksuit bottoms that fitted much better but he rushed up to me with a raft of other complaints.

There were similar problems with a prisoner who was 6ft 4in tall. His tracksuit trousers ended just below the knee and he looked ridiculous. A request for special kit should have gone out when he arrived at the jail. Some prisoners complained about the state of what they had to wear. 'Look' said one showing me his T shirt that was badly torn at the neck and hem. 'I've asked the officers about it, but they aren't interested.' I checked with staff that the prisoner hadn't torn it himself, and was told it was the fault of the laundry. It well might have been, but the prisoner still shouldn't have been given it to wear. Another T shirt was swiftly collected from stores and he felt much better. It was another small thing, easily solved that made a difference to the prisoner's self esteem.

Prisoners were supposed to hand back their used kit and bedclothes to officers in exchange for clean items. In practice, many didn't bother. As a result, there was often not enough clean kit to go round. The prison was jolted into action when it was discovered towards the end of 2013 that replacement kit was costing £4,000 a week instead of £4,000 a month. All prisoners were subsequently locked up while a cell search was undertaken. Piles of used kit were retrieved along with some illicit drugs and mobiles. One prisoner was allegedly found to have creatively made a makeshift sofa out of 23 blankets. All cells, which were either randomly selected or intelligence led were supposed to be searched on a three-month cycle. Staff liked prisoners to be present while they checked windows to ensure they were not being prepared for an escape, as well as the cells contents. Officers were also told to ask a prisoner if he had something that that shouldn't be there.

Officers were also supposed to go into every cell every day to check amongst other things that the emergency cell bell was working. At some point the blanket sofa would surely have been noticed. As it was no one seemed to know how this could have been allowed to happen.

CHAPTER THREE
LIFE ON THE WINGS I

I once counted the number of times I had locked and unlocked large heavy iron gates during an average morning's visit to the prison. It amounted to eighty-seven. On longer visits it must have been even more.

Anyone who arrived at the prison had to go through the manned gatehouse which was often a slow process. Although I had an identity badge and didn't have to provide any other form of documentation, there was just one queue for staff and visitors. Friends and family arriving for a social visit with a prisoner went through a separate entrance but often came to the gatehouse seeking information. No outsider can just walk into a prison. A Visiting Order has to be arranged in advance by the relevant internal department and given the OK by Security. When there were lots of visitors the gatehouse staff often struggled to find the relevant order from the pile.

Gatehouse personnel also checked credentials like passports and that visitors didn't have anything illegal with them. A list of prohibited items was on the wall close to the gatehouse hatch. It included obvious things like mobile phones and cameras, but also items like chewing gum, which could be used to make an imprint of prison keys, and atomizers, even handbag-size perfume ones, as these could be sprayed into an officer's eyes. Staff and monitors could leave their mobiles in a small outhouse in the prison grounds.

Although anyone on a social visit was scanned airport-style in a special room close by there was no scanning device at the gatehouse itself for daily use. Very occasionally the equipment was used for a spot-check on everyone else, including staff, but they were very time consuming and unlikely to take place when there were staff shortages. In my nearly ten years as a prison monitor it only happened once when I was at the prison. It doesn't seem anywhere near enough.

Once through the first gate, I then queued for prison keys. These couldn't under any circumstances be taken out from the prison, even for a moment. The security issue over keys was unconditional. In 2006 the Prison Service had to change 11,000 locks and 3,200 keys at Feltham Young Offenders' Institution after an ITV News camera lingered on a prison key. The shot was thought, by those who know, to have lasted long enough to enable a sharp-eyed criminal to remember the keys' shapes and indentations. The replacements were believed to have cost £250,000 but I don't know whether the Prison Service or the TV company paid the bill. Many thieves and safe-crackers have a photographic memory for key shapes, which was why I was told prison keys must never be obviously visible when I walked around the prison. Carrying loose keys was also forbidden as they could be grabbed by a prisoner. Instead they had to be clipped on to a thick chain and attached to a black belt I wore at all times once I left the gatehouse. At the end of 2013 the process for collecting keys was updated and a system that used individual fingerprints was installed. It made entering the prison more straightforward.

On the other side of Wormwood Scrubs' gatehouse and two other large iron gates were several flowerbeds. These were tended by prisoners who were trusted enough to work outside under the supervision of an officer. The plants were changed twice a year and added a splash of colour to the imposing building and the vast amounts of wire round its perimeter. Unfortunately the impact of the flowers was nearly always spoilt by masses of litter. Wormwood Scrubs has the dubious distinction of having been called 'the dirtiest prison in London'. One management figure once remarked ominously, 'There are no good dirty jails.'

The ground directly under cell windows was particularly unpleasant. The litter included discarded underwear, toilet paper, crisp wrappings, cake and biscuit packets, plastic bags, orange and banana peel, apple cores, half-eaten slices of bread, and occasionally human excrement. The litter covered wide areas and often became rain-sodden before it was removed. A group of prisoners known as Red Bands, who also had security clearance to work outside supervised by an officer, were paid about a pound a session to clear this up. A bio-hazard team had to deal with the excrement. As most prisoners didn't stay long there were often not enough of these trustworthy prisoners to do the work when it was needed. There might also not be enough staff to supervise them, or rain prevented the work being carried out. When the weather was bad for several days the grounds became a particularly disgusting sight. Nor was the work inspiring. The prisoners in the work party sometimes seemed to move in slow motion, and would sit around and chat at regular intervals. Progress was slow.

Not surprising the detritus was a haven for rats, mice, ravens and other predators. In 2011 the litter and vermin problem became so bad that the prison purchased a number of feral cats from a special charity to try to keep it under control. The animals were fed just enough to stop them getting lazy. I only saw them occasionally but obeyed the warnings on various gates and walls that they should not be touched or stroked.

The litter problem was caused entirely by prisoners who preferred to throw and push their rubbish through their cell windows to the ground below rather than place it in the bins in the wing. Notices on the wing boards warned that privileges might be stopped unless prisoners adopted better litter habits but it didn't seem to make any difference. An uncleared pile of litter about two foot deep was also the cause of a fire on a wing roof. Litter control was an ongoing battle for the monitors. We complained about it for years but it seemed to be a low-level priority for management

Internally some of the wings were often filthy too, despite the fact that they housed hundreds of prisoners with next to nothing to do. The floors were not too bad, but the metal stairs that lead from one level in the wing to another were thick with long-established grime, as usually was the area between the outer and inner door of each wing.

- - - - - - - -

Although Wormwood Scrubs, a category B prison, was a pioneering model of prison reform when it was built by convict labour in 1891, it was no longer an easy prison to run. Its physical shape is unwieldy, it has a wide range of prisoners and is a local prison with a constant turnover of inmates. It was originally designed in 1870s by Major-General Edmund Du Cane, chairman of the Directors of Convict Prisons and once it was finished became a local prison for short-term petty male and female offenders.

In 1902 the last female prisoner was transferred to HMP Holloway. From 1904, the prison became part of the Borstal system for young offenders. During World War II the prison was used by the War Department. In 1929 it was made an allocation centre from which newly-sentenced trainees were assessed before being sent to a suitable Borstal. It also specialised in holding first time offenders. During the Second World War, part of the prison was evacuated so it could be used by MI5 and the War Department. In the mid-1980s a £30.5m redevelopment scheme for the prison was approved and by 1994 a new hospital wing was completed. Two years later two of the four wings were refurbished, and a fifth wing completed.

There is now five main wings that hold between 176 and 330 prisoners plus a number of smaller dedicated units. The wings are separate from each other. There is no obvious centre to the jail and quite a walk to get from one end to the other. Wings often have a key purpose, but these change every few years, often it seemed when they were not functioning very well. For example all new prisoners were sent to one wing, then to another, then back to the first one and then finally to all of the wings. It never quite made sense.

A couple of wings contained both remand and convicted inmates, another those who had jobs within the prison. One wing held most of the addicts who required regular medication, another those who were mentally ill, had personality disorders, or were just difficult and needed to be in single cells. There was also a wing for those who were full-time workers or were preparing to leave the jail. It also housed any extra difficult prisoners. In addition there was a small super enhanced unit for prisoners considered to be trustworthy and who had key working roles within the prison. It was a disappointment to staff when a cache of illegal mobiles was found hidden in the unit at the beginning of 2014.

Because the prison was so old the central heating system was antiquated and either fully on or fully off. When the weather took an unseasonal turn the central heating took two or three days to catch up. This led to many complaints from the prisoners that they were freezing or too hot.

A hot summer was particularly difficult for those prisoners in the upper landings of wings where temperatures could soar unbearably. Animals wouldn't be allowed to be confined in such uncomfortable conditions but there was little available to help prisoners including those who were sharing cells. The windows were small and provided virtually no ventilation. I and others asked for fans but even before the swingeing cuts in 2013, we were told there was no budget for them and in any case fans couldn't be left in many prisoners' cells as they could be taken apart and used to self-harm or as a weapon.

The difference in atmosphere between the wings was obvious the moment I unlocked the wing gates. Prisoners created the mood, as did the staff. At any one time it could vary from relaxed and almost congenial to agitated and explosive, but the most overriding feeling was of impotence. Prison is the survival of the fittest. Day after day testosterone-fuelled young men were stuck in a narrow, claustrophobic, restrictive world. It often left them feeling passive and dependent or boiling over with frustration. Many of them became like needy little boys, albeit not always pleasant ones. If they shared a cell, as most did, they couldn't even go to the toilet in private. They had to ask for permission for almost everything from having a shower, to ringing their lawyer. They were, of course, in prison for a reason and the public must be protected, but a local prison like Wormwood Scrubs where most men served short sentences, puts humans on hold, increases the chance they will lose their homes, and encourages apathy especially if they are locked up most of the day, as there is insufficient time for them to build up skills that may help them live differently.

In November 2013 Lord Neuberger, president of the Supreme Court, questioned the value of short prison sentences, saying they could be 'disruptive' for the prisoner's job and family life and that if a prisoner needed help with substance abuse or training for a job the prison sentence needed to be at least six months. I believe prisons serve the purpose of removing criminals from society but that it needs a brave rethink for short-term offenders so that rather than being little more than a holding centre they offer something more positive.

– – – – – – – –

The shape of a prison day was necessarily rigid. Meals were served early, like they are in hospital, to fit in with officers' shifts. Lunch was at 11.30am and supper at 4.30pm. Breakfast-in-a-bag was served to prisoners after supper to eat whenever they chose. Mornings were supposed to be taken up with things like medical appointments, cleaning their cell, taking part in 'purposeful activity', legal visits, going to education and workshops or having a social visit. Afternoons were similar. There were also periods of association on the wing when as well as mixing with other prisoners, inmates had the chance of a shower, took exercise, played pool or used the phone on their landing.

People are fascinated by the secret world of prisons, but it takes a special kind of individual to want to work there. For many officers it was a vocation rather than a job. The salary, which is similar to a postman's, was modest and it was sometimes difficult to work out why anyone would want to put themselves constantly at risk of being physically assaulted by a prisoner, as well as deal with so many difficult and mentally ill inmates, without proper training. A position that could affect their own health. The level of violence was such that I doubt any of them escaped being attacked at least once in their career. It was important for me, as an independent monitor, not to be seen to get too friendly with officers, as prisoners could think my independence was compromised, but a few told me they worked in prisons because a close relative had a criminal record and they wanted to help others who had fallen foul of the law. A few enjoyed wielding power. The majority however would talk about how they wanted to keep prisoners 'safe'. They also thrived on not knowing what the next minute let alone the next day would bring and the challenges it would offer.

For the most part modern prison officers behaved more like social workers than guards, although one officer described himself as a mixture of social worker and Rambo. Another who worked on a wing full of demanding prisoners told me that he coped with them by thinking about his own children. 'I talk to inmates no matter what their age, like I used to when dealing with my sons when they were adolescents and playing up,' he said. 'I tell them off and explain that life would be easier for them when they behave. Many of them have never had a man in their lives who can be a role model, show them boundaries, or give them a different perspective on life. I like to think it can make a difference, even if only lasts for the time they are in here.' Equally there were also a minority of officers who liked to pull rank, and could be unhelpful and short tempered.

Over the years the numbers of female officers rose considerably at Wormwood Scrubs. Women have only been allowed to work in a male prison since 1987 but the public only seems to be aware of their existence when one of them hits the headlines by having illicit sex with one of the inmates. Females worked everywhere at Wormwood Scrubs including in the Segregation Unit. A senior governor told me he thought they 'helped make the place more civilized' and that prisoners behaved differently in front of them. Some were glamorous, others as if they had come from central casting and looked as tough as nails. I received several complaints from the prisoners about female staff who were 'cruel' or 'bullies' but never about those who were more motherly. 'Some of these lads have never been mothered' said one older officer. 'I make sure I look after them, but I don't take any nonsense. They are usually OK once they know the boundaries.' A few inmates made sexual advances towards members of the female staff. One wrote a letter telling an officer that he had 'strong feelings' for her. Others had serious issues about women. Badly mothered prisoners were often abusive to female officers or talked to them as if they were merely sexual objects. They were also sometimes attacked, spat at and punched. On one occasion a female officer had a fire extinguisher thrown at her head.

It made sense for offenders to have a courteous relationship with officers as they were a lifeline for information and help of all kinds. Independent monitors could concentrate fully on specific individuals who sought assistance on something specific a few days a month, but prison officers were always there and dealt with hundreds of men who wanted attention.

The sometimes curious inter-dependent relationship between prisoner and officer could help a prisoner survive in jail and, as strange as it sounds, also contribute towards the safe and smooth running of a wing. Twenty or so years ago there could be around thirty prison officers to a wing. They would stay in one post for a number of years, get to know the prisoners and they would get to know him. They even helped prisoners fill out legal aid forms, change solicitors and tell them what to expect in the courts. By 2011 the numbers of officers per wing had been reduced to about twelve but most remained allocated to one wing and could still spot if a prisoner was getting depressed or suicidal, keep an eye on a volatile prisoner's moods and defuse signs of aggression before they spilt over. It also meant that reclusive prisoners who withdrew from the prison regime were less likely to be forgotten. Equally, if a prisoner wanted to seek help they could approach the officer on a landing. This altered in October 2013 following the massive policy change.

Physical assaults were part and parcel of prison life and Ministry of Justice figures show that the number of reported assaults in London's male prisons rose by a third in four years from 1,463 in 2007 to 1,950, in 2011. In one randomly-picked month on one wing, officers had to deal with the following: an attack when an officer nearly lost an eye and was hospitalised, a threat by a prisoner with a razorblade, verbal threats by three prisoners, a prisoner who refused to be searched following a visit and had to be restrained, four fights between four sets of prisoners one of which took place in the exercise yard and one in the shower and a prisoner running from the chapel to one of the outer corners of the prison. In addition two prisoners self-harmed by cutting their arms badly, there was one death in custody and two prisoners tried to hang themselves by using ligatures, eight mobiles were found in cells plus a charger and USB, and there were three drug finds. Other violence on a different wing included: a prisoner wrapping his arms in toilet paper and setting himself on fire, a prisoner biting an officer on the leg, a prisoner head butting an officer, breaking an officer's finger, throwing boiling water over an officer, fighting another prisoner over the pool table, a fight between inmates serving lunch, two prisoners setting fire to their cells and one setting fire to bedding.

- - - - - - - -

Some prisons operate a personal officer's scheme where specific officers are responsible for individual prisoners. It is a potentially good idea for large prisons as it offers consistency for prisoners. Wormwood Scrubs did not have named personal officers; instead it maintained that all officers should be responsible for all prisoners on their wing. I felt it was unrealistic to expect that in a busy prison with sometimes more than three hundred prisoners to a wing that every officer would be able to dedicate the same amount of time to all the prisoners when none had been specially selected for him. The prison has been criticised for this stand by government inspectors, the Prisons and Probation Ombudsman, and coroners.

Staff were expected to show prisoners respect by addressing them as Mister followed by their surname. Prisoners on the other hand largely called staff by their first names. I thought it was a phony unbalanced gesture towards prisoners and that both prisoners and staff should address each other in the same manner. I suspect monitors were supposed to do the same, but I avoided the issue by not using the prisoner's name, except when checking how it was spelt. I felt it was much more important to listen to his problems and try to help him. I didn't mind how inmates addressed me. Some called me by my first name, which they saw on my identification badge. Most seemed to prefer 'Miss'.

Very occasionally, however, the relationship between staff and prisoner became toxic and an officer was persuaded to traffic drugs or mobiles. It could also happen as a result of grooming. A prisoner could claim to know where the officer lived and where his or her children went to school and make threats that unless they brought in contraband the children would suffer. It is perhaps not surprising that with about 25,000 prison officers working in over 130 prisons in England and Wales that there would inevitably be an occasional black sheep.

Prisoners also made regular complaints about some officers. 'When I speak to some of the prison staff it is like talking to a brick wall,' one explained. Unfortunately, despite my best efforts to sort out these type of complaints, I failed to get very far. My own experience was that while most officers were very helpful there were a few who were not. I didn't take it personally, but staff are obliged to help independent monitors, who, after all, are appointed by the Ministry of Justice. I also noticed that when it came down to an officer's word against a prisoner it was more likely that the officer's word would be taken.

Prisoners' complaints about staff were processed in a different way to general complaints. Instead of going in the green box they came directly to the Chair of the monitors on a pink form labelled 'confidential complaint'. These became my responsibility once I took over as Chair in January 2011. Allegations included being sexually assaulted, physically attacked, victimised or deliberately not being given a job within the prison by various officers.

The prisoner who alleged sexual assault could offer no evidence, nor a witness. Another prisoner in the Segregation Unit alleged that an officer punched him ferociously in the face that morning. 'Can you see anything?' he asked. I couldn't. 'There must be a red mark somewhere.' There wasn't. I suggested he filled in a complaints form. 'I won't do that' he replied. 'I've been working and don't want to get the sack. But you could complain for me.'

Prisoners couldn't be relied on to tell the truth, but nor could it be assumed they always lied. They could be manipulative, have a personal agenda or have taken against an officer for a whole range of reasons including not letting them do something that was against prison rules. Nor could a clutch of similar complaints from a variety of prisoners in the same wing against the same officer be taken at face value. A strong-minded prisoner could persuade or bully other prisoners to follow his lead purely to get his own back on an officer or make his or her life difficult. I once received six almost identically written complaints including the same spelling mistakes and in the same handwriting about a named officer from one wing accusing him of bringing in drugs and mobile phones. It was a suspicious co-ordination to say the least.

However, virtually every prisoner who was keen to recount lurid tales of an officer's bullying and intolerable abuse and how his life was a nightmare, refused point blank to allow his name to go forward as the instigator of the complaint. Instead, each of them wanted me to accept what he had said at face value. The policy of the Scrubs, however, was that an officer had the right to know from the start not just the details of any complaint but the name of the individual who was complaining about him. This always seemed unfair not least because prisoners feared they would be targeted by the officer in question, often in subtle ways like being unlocked last for meals, which meant there was little or no choice, or when there was social time. I understood that the identity of the prisoner had to be revealed at some stage so the officer could defend himself, I just didn't feel it should be done right at the start.

At one point I started compiling a confidential blacklist of the names of officers prisoners had complained about over a relatively long period to see if the same names cropped up. They did, so I passed the officers' names on to a senior member of staff but didn't include any prisoners' names. I heard by chance several months later that one of the officers on the list had been moved from the wing to another job within the prison, which may or may not have been a coincidence.

In 2013, however, two prisoners not only made two serious complaints about a member of staff, they also agreed to allow their names to go forward. I passed everything on to someone senior in the prison but heard nothing for several weeks. After pushing the matter I was told an investigation had been done and nothing was found to have been out of order. I then discovered that both prisoners had been moved to other prisons. The move may well have had nothing to do with their complaints. I had no evidence to prove otherwise, but I was left with an uncomfortable feeling.

In both 2012 and 2013 I wrote about how difficult it was to deal with prisoners' complaints about staff in the Annual Report that monitoring boards submit to the Justice Secretary. I wrote that I was uneasy about how these investigations were conducted and that in my view they lacked transparency. It was one item in a much larger report and not referred to in correspondence from the Prison Minister. It was frustrating that I could highlight issues but had no power to change them. The prison attitude towards complaints about a very small number of staff seems particularly inappropriate, as in the past trouble of all sorts in Wormwood Scrubs helped to secure the jail's notoriety.

-- -- -- -- --

In 1966, the spy George Blake climbed to freedom over a Scrub's wall. He had been sentenced to 42 years in prison and was closely guarded, but he constructed an audacious plan that involved a ladder made from rope and size 13 knitting needles. In today's prison no prisoner would be allowed to have knitting needles. In 1979 IRA protesters staged a rooftop protest over visiting rights. There were also serious disturbances inside the jail including a sit-in by sixty inmates in the then lifers' wing who protested about a range of issues including the quality of toiletries they were permitted to buy. The prison toothpaste in particular was described as so gritty and bitter it 'ripped your mouth to shreds.' Internal discord was rife and shortly afterwards there was an explosive riot in which sixty inmates and several prison officers were injured.

Shortly afterwards a new governor, John McCarthy, was shipped in following his success as Governor of Cardiff prison. He was so disturbed by the overcrowding of the prison and what he believed was the lack of interest by the then home secretary William Whitelaw, that he sent a furious letter to The Times in 1981 describing himself as 'the manager of a large penal dustbin.' He resigned soon afterwards. His successor, Ian Dunbar, had to cope with riots and violence throughout 1983.

During the 1980s the prison's monitoring board, then called the board of visitors, continually criticised the prison over its poor standards of hygiene and lack of decent provision for the mentally ill. Its report of August 1987 described a 'desolate regime' and said that 'nothing has changed since our report last year – despite reassurances that things would change.' In 1989, it declared that the sex offender annex was 'out of control', that the inmates were more likely to reoffend once released and expressed concerns over the safety of staff.

In 1998 a dossier was compiled of allegations against staff. This was followed by a secret report by the Prison Service in 2004 that uncovered a 'nine-year reign of terror' at Wormwood Scrubs. It included many incidents that the prison had publicly refused to admit and highlighted that more than 160 prison officers between 1992 and 2001 were involved in covering up what was described as a 'regime of torture' which included 'savage beatings, death threats and sexual assaults inflicted on inmates.' It branded the terror as the worst case of prisoner abuse in modern history. In addition, managers blatantly falsified records. For example, paperwork on the day of one assault shows the names of the staff on duty being recorded as officers 'Nobody, Invisible, Non-existent and Absent.' The review concluded an inquiry should be held, but, that decision was overturned by the then Home Secretary, David Blunkett, a position his successors have stuck to. It finally resulted in 27 officers being suspended. Three of them were subsequently convicted of violence against prisoners.

In 2001 government inspectors felt the prison had not yet been restored to an effective and healthy state. An inspection in 2008 noted improvements but in 2010 the monitoring board believed that prison life was on the decline, ironically this time due to financial and staff cutbacks rather than poor staff attitudes. Three years earlier on 29 August 2007 a significant number of prison officers and particularly those who belonged to the Prison Officers Association (POA) started its first ever national strike. A group of officers gathered at the prison gate to try to persuade their colleagues not to go in for their shifts. The prison immediately shut down, prisoners were confined to their cells and couldn't go to court, while exercise and all activities including social visits were cancelled. This was particularly distressing for those family members and friends who had travelled considerable distances to see a prisoner. The safety and running of the prison was left to eight governors and a handful of administrators from Prison Service headquarters who weren't qualified to unlock cell doors. If there had been a serious emergency, it could have been a disaster.

The Ministry of Justice said the walk-out was a breach of the Industrial Relations Act but Jack Straw then Home Secretary, claimed contingency plans were in place to maintain security. I went into the prison around lunchtime to see if the prisoners had been fed. Governors were taking a cold meal to each cell and the prisoners to whom I spoke through the cracks in their doors seemed calm about the situation. I walked round the inner yard of the prison close to the wing walls to see if all was well, when suddenly some liquid was thrown on me from an upper cell. It happened so quickly that I didn't see exactly which cell it came from. Nor could I judge whether it was water or urine. I cringed. Almost immediately a prisoner I couldn't see shouted from the direction the liquid had come: 'You fucking idiot! She's here to help us. She's not an officer. So sorry, Miss. I've told who done (sic) it off and I'll get him for you. He didn't realise who you were.' I went home and had a long shower. I never found out who did it. By the time I went back into the prison, I couldn't quite remember the location of the cell and the perpetrator hadn't been reported. I have never walked under the cell windows since.

A court injunction was sought and the strike finished in the early afternoon. In January 2008, the Home Secretary announced plans to reintroduce powers to ban strikes by prison officers in England and Wales, but four years later on 10 May 2012 the POA called a five-hour strike in protest against government-imposed changes to the Civil Service pension scheme. Governors were taken 'completely by surprise' when the strike was announced at 6.30am. Prison staff start early and most of the governing grades were already in. They discussed managing essential services, including supplying methadone to those with drug issues. In contrast to the strike in 2008, the governors managed to get prisoners ready to be taken to court, and to discharge those who had completed their sentence that day. Prisoners were told that they wouldn't get exercise or any other activities and social visits were cancelled. A cold lunch was served at 1pm, ninety minutes later than usual. One prisoner in the first-night centre was very distraught that his visit wouldn't take place, and another set fire to his cell, which may or may not have had anything to do with the strike. He was taken to the Segregation Unit. Otherwise everything was calm. Staff returned to work just before the injunction was scheduled to be heard in court.

- - - - - - - -

The incident with the liquid reinforced the importance of staying safe and reminded me of the chance of trouble flaring up in an instant. It also made me think more about the possibility of being taken hostage. During my training I had been told that the prison responded differently to a prison officer being taken hostage than if the hostage was a monitor. Officers were expected to take responsibility for themselves if they were captured and barricaded in a cell so prisoners wouldn't believe that by capturing an officer they could negotiate a deal. This wasn't the case with monitors. The prison would, we were told, do what it could to release us so we should bear in mind that we were, at least in theory, more at risk. Fortunately, it never happened.

Prison officers came into their own when there was trouble in a wing and as far as I saw dealt with it quickly, professionally, in a controlled manner and by the book. If they needed extra help from another wing they rang the alarm bell. It was very different to being somewhere when the fire alarm goes off and you are never quite sure whether the equipment was merely being tested or it was a genuine alarm. In the Scrubs officers immediately stopped what they were doing and raced to the troubled wing. Monitors were encouraged to stay and watch to see that disturbances were handled humanely – we could be called as witnesses if prisoners made allegations against officers – but we had to stand at a safe distance from any trouble.

I was in one wing when a prisoner on the first landing barricaded himself behind his cell door. The alarm went off, the wing shut down and I was told that if I wanted to stay I had to go to the fourth landing where I would be safe and have a good view of the incident. A couple of officers talked to the prisoner through the door in a firm but calm and conciliatory manner. They seemed experts at defusing the crisis. Meanwhile another group of officers kitted out in riot gear, helmets and see-through shields, lined up along the wall close to the cell but out of the sight of the prisoner. I presumed this was in case they had to storm the cell. While this was going on those prisoners who were coming back from the gym and visits were taken one by one to their cells. After about thirty minutes the prisoner removed the barricade, his cell door was opened and he was escorted calmly to the Segregation Unit by the four officers in riot gear, whom he looked astonished to see.

There were prescribed ways for an officer to handle this type of situation. They were encouraged to use common sense and not put themselves in danger. It meant that if there was a fight, even just between two prisoners, they should judge whether they needed back-up before getting involved. They could use force but no more than was 'reasonable.' The reasonableness was judged on each set of circumstances. If they used more force than was necessary, it could be declared unlawful. This placed enormous pressure on officers, who had to make split-second decisions in a stressful situation, but they seemed used to it. Officers who needed to use force were encouraged to adopt what is called Control and Restraint techniques, but they could only be used if three or more officers were present, as each of them was responsible for tackling one part of the prisoner's body and effectively immobilising him with a few simple but effective movements.

When there was a significant disturbance the prison's Command Suite was opened in a designated room in the administrative block. This happened whenever a prisoner jumped on the netting between two wing landings and refused to come down. It would be described as a bronze, silver or gold incident depending on its seriousness and a multi-disciplinary team would form to deal with the situation. It sometimes took several hours to persuade the prisoner to come down. Most of them were subsequently transferred to another prison.

Independent monitors were always informed when one of these incidents happened and had a duty to go into the prison, observe what was going on and, without getting in the way, take notes and write a report. Violent incidents at Wormwood Scrubs increased from October 2013.

If, and this never happened during my time at Wormwood Scrubs, an incident turned into a full-blown riot, the prison could call on an outside specialist Tornado Unit to help them. This group of men included officers who had completed an advanced Control and Restraint training. The Tornados would turn up to a serious incident with riot helmet, flame-retardant overalls and balaclava, gloves, belt, side-arm baton and holder, shin guards, elbow protectors, boots, and shield. A Tornado team was used at Maidstone Prison, Kent, in November 2013 to bring a riot under control. The Prison Service said forty inmates took part but officers told the media it had involved up to 180 prisoners. A Tornado team was also sent to Oakwood Prison near Wolverhampton, Britain's biggest privately-run jail, that can accommodate 1,600 prisoners, to handle a riot in January 2014.

This was also downplayed. G4S, who run the prison, described it as a small incident involving fifteen or twenty prisoners. An officer who helped deal with the incident said it was in fact a 'full-scale riot': inmates had taken over an entire wing and booby-trapped the doorways in a nine-hour stand-off. It was an example of the over-optimistic 'good news' culture the Government and Prison Service are prone to operate.

I went to see the Tornados training at a secret location. It was fascinating to watch how they dealt with mock scenarios like coping with a fire – they had to walk through flames to show they had faith in their flame-proof overalls – and severe disruption on a wing.

- - - - - - - -

Day in day out officers aimed to keep prisoners safe, calm and engaged with the regime. Sharing a cell with a prisoner could make a substantial difference to how a prisoner coped, so the mix in a double cell was thought about carefully. Prisoners who spoke the same language were put together, as were non-smokers. If the cell sharing didn't work, officers tried to change the arrangement. Some prisoners were quite fussy. 'Why I have to force to stay with someone (sic)', a non-English prisoner wrote to me.

Some of the most relaxed prisoners were those who had another family member in jail with them. Over time I met brothers, cousins, uncles and nephews, father and sons, and even one grandfather and grandson who were in Wormwood Scrubs together. It was a visual rather than statistical proof of how crime travelled from generation to generation in some families to become a way of life. The family members who talked to me seemed quite undisturbed about being in jail. Their major concern was that if one of them was transferred to another prison the other went too.

One prisoner wrote how distraught he was that his father had been transferred to another jail, leaving him alone at Wormwood Scrubs: 'I request your humble assistance in reuniting a heartbroken son with his loving father.' Another son who shared a cell with his ailing father seemed to be a doting carer; his focus was on doing everything he could to relieve his father's chronic medical condition. The prison was remarkably adaptable on this matter.

CHAPTER FOUR
LIFE ON THE WINGS II

Those who needed a sympathetic ear during their imprisonment could also turn to the chaplaincy. Every prison has a chaplaincy department and at Wormwood Scrubs they worked as a multi-faith team. It meant in practice that a Muslim imam could visit a Roman Catholic, Jewish or Church of England prisoner to give him pastoral care. Chaplains tried to see all prisoners within 48 hours of their arrival. Prisoners weren't obliged to register their religion and could change it at any time. A member of the chaplaincy would visit prisoners in the Segregation Unit and Healthcare every day as well as seeing prisoners on the general wings. In the early 2000s there was a substantial chaplaincy team that included full-time Anglican, Catholic, Muslim and Church of English chaplains plus several part-timers and sessional chaplains for less represented religions. From 2011 this was partially cut back in line with the reduced prison budget but while the number of imams increased to two full-time and two part-timers, Christians lost out. Between 2012 and 2013 there was no Church of England chaplain at all. One of the chaplaincy team thought it was not right: 'The Church of England does represent the established religion of the country after all.' By 2014 there were only two full-time chaplains, an Anglican and a Muslim, with a few others coming in for specific sessions.

The full-time chaplains gave advice on religious matters throughout the prison. The imam also advised Muslim prisoners on how to cope when they were strip-searched. Islam doesn't allow individuals to be naked in front of anyone other than their spouse, but this can be overridden under certain circumstances. It was a similar situation when Muslims were in the presence of the sniffer dog looking for drugs – the saliva of a dog is considered to be impure.

I saw one Muslim prisoner shortly after he had been taken to the Segregation Unit. A drug search with dogs had been launched during Ramadan and he had been caught with cannabis. 'How dare they put dogs on me especially when I am fasting?' he said as if he bore no responsibility for the situation he found himself in. 'Dogs are not allowed to touch me, but they went for my groin and back, and I now have three nickings for cannabis.' A nicking is prison-speak for a disciplinary charge. The officer who opened his cell door told me the prisoner was also charged with threatening to kill the dog handler and the dog.

It was often difficult, as a woman, to help an intense Islamist and I had one particularly unpleasant experience. I had taken an application out of the locked green box on the wing wall and went to find the prisoner who had written it. He was a foreign national and although his written English wasn't very good, it was clear he was dissatisfied with how he was being treated. It was mid-morning, many of the prisoners were out and about, and he wasn't in his cell. I asked a member of staff if he was still in the wing or had gone for a legal visit or education – all prisoners who leave a wing are logged out and then back in again when they return so there is always an up-to-date record of where everyone is. I wasn't told anything about his behaviour, just that he had remained on the wing. I asked for him to be called on the wing Tannoy.

He was obviously quite angry when he arrived to meet me, jabbed his finger at the written application and instructed me in no uncertain terms what I had to do. It was quite a list and included photocopying various documents he had in his cell, and then posting them to his lawyer. Although I explained I was happy to help a prisoner fill out a form, his demands were outside my boundary as a prison monitor because we couldn't provide office services. Nor I explained could we post anything for a prisoner. I decided not to add that any letter could contain illicit material or be sent to intimidate a witness. I could however help if he felt he was being unfairly treated within the prison. Otherwise he needed to ask a prison officer what to do. He was furious, raised his voice and looked at me venomously. There was something about him that was so disturbing that I instinctively felt, for the first and only time in prison, that I could be attacked. I quickly make an excuse and left the wing.

I went straight to the administrative office that dealt with foreign nationals to find out more about him. As I walked through the door I saw the prisoner's name and number written in red ink on the white notice board together with a written warning that he was a potential danger to all and especially to women. A member of staff told me he didn't like being told what to do by a woman, that he had spat at a female officer recently and assaulted another when she had asked him to return to his cell. He was waiting to be deported. I was also told that there was a 'risk to staff' register that gave details of prisoners like him that everyone should be wary of and that those who were particularly dangerous to women were listed separately.

Although it had been my fault not to check on him with a wing officer before we spoke I felt monitors like me should be warned in advance about potentially dangerous prisoners. No one had mentioned that there was a list of these men regularly emailed to various departments. No one had thought to send it to the monitors, but as we dealt with prisoners on an individual basis I asked for this to be changed. After this experience before going into a wing I always checked the 'risk to staff register.'

It was not surprising that the Imam was a high-profile figure around the jail. Ministry of Justice figures revealed that Muslim prisoners numbered 3,681 in 1997 and 11,278 in 2012, an increase from one in 16 of the prison population to one in seven. A MoJ source commented : 'This is mainly because of the number of foreign nationals in UK jails but is also affected by religious conversion." Meanwhile the number of inmates who declared that they were Church of England dropped from 23,209 in 2008 to 18,896 in 2012. Muslim prisoners were also more likely to go to religious services. In one randomly selected month the number of Muslims who attended prayers was 830, compared to 531 Catholics and 484 Church of England. Although a few prisoners told me they went to religious services to get out of their cells and mix with other prisoners, many took the services seriously, and two extra imams came to help with Friday prayers. Because of the high numbers the services had to be divided between the gym and multi-faith chapel. The gym was very popular with prisoners and there were complaints that they couldn't exercise there on a Friday because of the prayers. There was, however, nowhere else in the prison large enough to hold all the Muslim worshippers.

- - - - - - - -

It is well-known that people often turn to religion in prison because they are going through a difficult time in their lives and many are drawn into a rigid ideology. It might have been the location of Wormwood Scrubs or the unique mix of the prisoners but not once did a prisoner tell me that he had become a Christian or Roman Catholic whilst in jail, but prisoners regularly stated they had found salvation by converting to Islam. One summed it up. He said: 'I am nearly 50 years old and have been in trouble since I was 18. But I have turned my life around now I am a Muslim and am praying five times a day.'

There were some hard-core Muslim fundamentalists in Wormwood

Scrubs, who were waiting to be deported. The men wore traditional clothing and, it seemed, kept themselves aloof from their fellow inmates. In such a vast establishment it was difficult for me to be aware of any prisoners who were being 'groomed'.

One senior staff member said that prisoners were encouraged to convert but that it was done in a 'subtle' way. 'It goes on all the time, but the top brass pretend it isn't happening because they just don't want to know,' he said. Another officer thought it was ironic that it was becoming increasingly common as a result of Prime Minister David Cameron's Extremism Task Force. This was set up in the wake of the murder of drummer Lee Rigby in May 2013. Based on its recommendations, hundreds of Muslim clerics were enlisted to help deradicalise Islamist extremists in British jails. The officer I spoke to added: 'The Government is so concerned about tackling extremism that resources have been spent flooding prisons with imams to explain to prisoners that Islam isn't just about suicide bombers. They are supposed to counter the extremists but in fact the prisoners relate to imams because they are the ones who are most around. A prisoner starts talking to an imam who seems sympathetic and non-judgmental and thinks that if he is so nice, perhaps there is something in the religion. It gives them something new to think about, and probably for the first time in their lives they find structure and guidance. They are also being offered something that costs nothing to join. The conversion happens by osmosis.'

Some prisoners worried about this too. Several who shared a cell with a prisoner who was converting alerted security about what was going on. One prisoner reported his cellmate to staff when he grew a beard and began waking him up at 3am when he prayed. Another worried that his cellmate was being radicalised because he was spending so much time reading the Koran.

Many Muslim prisoners did not think they were treated well in Wormwood Scrubs. The Chief Inspector of Prisons wrote in his 2011 report on Wormwood Scrubs that Muslim prisoners reported negatively across a range of issues. 'More Muslim than other prisoners said they had been subject to use of force and more said they had been segregated overnight. Fewer said there was a member of staff they could turn to for help and fewer said most staff treated them with respect. Only 19%, compared to 37% of non-Muslims, said they were currently working.' He added: 'Despite these differences of perception, many aspects of religious diversity were well managed, including arrangements for Ramadan.'

One Muslim, a first-timer in prison in his twenties, was determined never to come back. 'I have had a rough time in prison,' he confessed. 'When I get out, I am going to live in Jamaica with my mum. I have three children, two from the same mum. They will stay in the UK. I am not a good role model but I keep telling myself that I can turn away from crime.' Another feared for his life: 'My life's in danger and I might commit suicide or kill someone. I am in prison to be looked after, not discriminated against.'

Like all prisons, Wormwood Scrubs worked towards eradicating discrimination against prisoners on the grounds of race, religion, or sexual inclination, but these types of complaints could take an interminable time to process. 'The procedures can drive anyone barmy,' an officer agreed. He also believed much more credence was given to prisoners who made racial complaints about staff than the other way round. 'A Muslim lad became very volatile when an officer was helping serve the meal because his halal choice wasn't available. He stared at the officer, then called him a racist cunt and a white fucker. The officer challenged him verbally but not physically and said how dare he use that sort of language. He then asked another officer to come with him to take the prisoner back to his cell in an effort to de-escalate the tension. Before he went into the cell the prisoner raised his voice and stepped towards the officer. He gave him a clear direct order not to come any closer but he didn't listen. The officer then pushed him away, the prisoner punched him so the officer pushed him into his cell and locked the door. Shortly afterwards the prisoner claimed the officer had assaulted him and the officer was suspended for six months. Nothing was done about the prisoner's racist language, some of us felt, because the officer was white.' It did seem at times that the powers that be, whether instructed to or not, tiptoed round certain issues with Muslims as avoiding being accused of racism was a priority.

-- -- -- -- -- -- --

Homophobia was equally frowned on but the gay prisoners I met preferred to keep a low profile. Sexual relations between prisoners and staff were banned, but those between prisoners were usually quietly ignored. Condoms were available but only about twelve were given out per month. The low uptake either indicated that there was not much demand or that prisoners were not using protection. One gay prisoner asked to see me because he felt vulnerable. 'I believe I am being discriminated against because of my sexual orientation,' he complained. 'There is a lot of homophobia here and when people call me names no member of staff deals with it. I had been hiding my sexual orientation for a long time, because I felt ashamed and I have only just come out.' I suggested he put in a confidential complaint to the Governor.

Two transgender prisoners stayed at different times at Wormwood Scrubs. When they arrived staff who would be in contact with them were given special training. One of the prisoners, who was on hormone treatment, was put in the Segregation Unit for her own protection. She was in a sorry state, had serious drug issues and kept throwing food around. She complained about the shower facilities and wearing prison-issue clothes. The Unit was patently not suitable for her but she refused to engage in the prison regime as she was scared of being surrounded by men, so it would have been inappropriate to put her on a wing. She was kept safe until she could be transferred to somewhere more suitable.

Even straightforward relationships could cause problems. One prisoner insisted he knew both his rights and details of the relevant prison service orders that govern how the prison should be run. 'My girlfriend is in another prison and we want to marry via videolink,' he told me. 'It is a human right as long as you are both convicted and both give consent. I would like you to help arrange the wedding as soon as possible because her prison is bad at that sort of thing. I have money for the registrar and my birth certificate is lying on my bed.' I explained I wasn't able to deal with issues outside the prison but I would check on the relevant prison service order for him. I found it wasn't an absolute right to marry in jail: it was up to the Governor whether or not a marriage could take place. Nor was a chaplain obliged to perform a civil ceremony.

I can't remember a visit to the prison that didn't include at least one prisoner talking about his rights. Their human rights involved everything from food, showers and clean clothing to drugs and work. But not once did any of them mention the right to vote.

In December 2013 the European Court of Human Rights ruled the UK's current ban on prisoner voting was unlawful. It said the vote should 'not be removed without good reason' but conceded that those guilty of 'heinous crimes' should be disenfranchised. In response, a cross-party committee of MPs and peers recommended that prisoners serving jail terms of a year or less and those coming to the end of their sentence should be entitled to vote.

I did a personal poll whenever the subject hit the headlines: I asked every prisoner I came across over several weeks for their view. I did not include foreign nationals, as they would not be able to vote. It was by no means scientific but not one of them was remotely interested. Their comments about politicians were confined to abusive four-letter words.

CHAPTER FIVE
THE SEGREGATION UNIT

The Segregation Unit was home to the mad, bad and, ironically, the most vulnerable prisoners. It was a small unit with sparse single cells where prisoners were kept in solitary confinement, locked up with no one but themselves for company for 23 hours a day. They were allowed out one at a time to collect their meals that were served within the unit. When I first became a monitor there was a reluctance to provide furniture in the Seg cells because prisoners broke it when they lost their temper or would try, for example, to use a table leg as a weapon. They had to eat their meals with the plate on their lap, on the bed or on the floor. After constant pressure and the support and action of a few governors cardboard furniture was eventually ordered. It wouldn't appear in House and Garden, but did make the cell slightly more civilised.

The unit housed paedophiles and those criminals who had committed serious offences including terrorists and serial murderers. They were kept in isolation for their own safety until a more suitable prison was found. This also applied to those whose crimes had hit the headlines, or if they were well known. It could take days, weeks or occasionally months to find a suitable prison that had space. In February 2014, prisons across the country were so full a selection of these men were stuck for many weeks in the Segregation Unit.

The Segregation Unit was also home for those who were vulnerable and easily bullied. Many prisons have dedicated vulnerable prisoner units but Wormwood Scrubs does not. Instead these vulnerable men were placed in solitary confinement amongst the most violent and disturbed men in the jail. Some of them were addicts who owed money to drug dealers in the prison and feared for their lives. In a violence reduction survey conducted within the prison the majority of prisoners believed that debts, which could be directly linked to drug use, were most likely to lead to violence. Frustration and boredom was also mentioned and was another cause of violence towards staff.

The Seg was also a dumping ground for the mentally ill when there was no room for them in the small healthcare unit. It was difficult to think of a more inappropriate environment even for those who were prone to violence. There were also prisoners who had been caught with illegal items in their cells, for example mobile phones, those who had been in fights with other prisoners or staff, those who refused to obey a prison officer's order, smashed up their cell or were too wild or anti-social to stay in a normal wing. It was also where newly arrived troublemakers and gang leaders were put when they had instigated violence at other prisons and the governor of that prison wanted them out as soon as possible. It was an arrangement that was reciprocated when Wormwood Scrubs wanted to get rid of a particularly tricky criminal. In fact there were a small group of violent or damaged men with so many issues that prisons found them extremely difficult to cope with and they would be transported round various jails like unwanted baggage.

The Segregation Unit also contained a special accommodation unit for those who were on a dirty protest. This was a horrifyingly popular anti-social degrading act for desperate and troubled men. If they failed to get their own way and felt unable to express themselves verbally, they protested by spreading excrement over the walls of their cells and often themselves.

Like much about the prison, I could never anticipate what a visit to the Seg would reveal. It could be quiet or have one or more prisoners constantly ringing the alarm bell in their cell - all cells had them in case of an emergency – or banging on the cell door sometimes for hours on end. One prisoner was told off firmly by an officer who said: 'Ringing your bell because you have some rubbish in your cell is not an emergency.'

The number, type of prisoners as well as the atmosphere in the unit could, like a wing, change from one minute to the next so it was important to monitor what was going on and every prison visit I made included a visit to the Segregation Unit. It was always well staffed by a bunch of exceptional men and women officers who were skilled at treading the difficult line between maintaining discipline and order with remarkable understanding, tolerance and compassion. The statement of intent for the Unit was: 'to manage difficult and refractory prisoners in a humane and progressive manner working with them to address their social behaviour and enabling them to return to normal location' (main wings). An officer put it another way. 'Our routine is set in stone here. If they cooperate they will be fine.'

When a prisoner arrived he was looked at closely and any scratches and bruises noted down in case he tried to blame the marks on the officers in the unit. It was wise to stay one step ahead of the prisoner. A doctor visited the prisoners every day as did one of the prison governors and a chaplain. The compulsory minimum of thirty minutes a day exercise for prisoners also applied to those in the Seg and took place in the small adjacent yard outside the unit. It did though depend on the weather. Few healthy men would think twice about going out in rainy or frosty conditions, but letting prisoners out in the wrong type of weather could have significant financial implications.

Canny prisoners were always on the look out for opportunities to claim 'compensation'. Slipping on frosty or wet ground had the potential of being turned into a nice little earner. Not surprisingly officers veered on the side of caution. It was a strange kind of cosseting especially if the prisoner was as big as a bear. The prisoners were rarely allowed out together. Some were too violent or vulnerable to mix with other men and all of them were given a thorough body search before and after they went outside. They seldom took advantage of the small opportunity to get themselves fit. Instead they either slowly idled around the yard, sat with their backs to the wall or stood staring at the middle distance.

- - - - - - - -

Because the prisoners in the Seg were often difficult, dangerous or mentally disturbed, it was important to keep meticulous notes of everything that happened and everyone who came in and out. There was always a large amount of paperwork to deal with at every visit. The nature of some of the inmates was also why some officers regularly suggested monitors talked to prisoners through a crack in the locked cell door rather than face to face. Some monitors were happy doing this, but I don't think you can effectively communicate that way or see the state of a cell, and unless they were extremely dangerous, I asked for each cell door to be unlocked so I could see each prisoner properly. Because it was important to be neutral about a prisoner, I didn't look up his crime until after I had seen him and sometimes not at all. My role was more focused on what was happening now.

An easy but not foolproof way of judging how dangerous a prisoner might be was whether officers said one, two or three officers needed to be present when the cell was unlocked. The more officers who stood guard the more unpredictable the prisoner was. But not always. I remember a prisoner who had been dragged to the Segregation Unit after exploding with rage and hurling a chair at a valuable stained glass window in the prison chapel, a valued grade 2 listed building. The window, which was 150 years old, was smashed and I was told would cost at least £5,000 to fix. I arrived at the unit shortly after he had been brought in by a specially trained team of four officers. An officer said it was a three-man unlock, that he was very dangerous and spoke no English so it was a waste of time seeing him. The point of being an independent monitor rather than being employed by the prison was that officers couldn't tell me who I may and may not talk to and I always felt it was an essential part of the job to see those who were under stress.

Somewhat reluctantly they opened the cell door. The prisoner was pacing the cell and obviously distraught but it didn't take me long to discover that although he didn't speak English he could speak French, a language I am familiar with. He had been picked up five days earlier brought to the prison and basically left to himself. It was prison practice to provide induction sessions for new prisoners within a day of their arrival and to find an interpreter if they were not English speaking so that they were made aware of prison rules and procedures. For reasons unknown he'd missed this and no one had communicated with him during his five days in jail.

His told me that his wife and parents had no idea where he was, that no one had offered him an opportunity to ring them, which again was his right to do, and he had burst with frustration in the chapel that morning. He apologized and offered to pay for the damage caused. He then showed me a letter he wanted to send to his wife and another to his lawyer. They were both literate and well expressed and I suggested he give them to one of the officers to send to the post room. I also asked for a French speaker to come to the Segregation unit that day to tell him how the prison operated. He duly did and when I came along to see him a couple of days later he was calm and no longer a threat. The same can't be had for one prisoner who was seriously unstable and volatile. 'The trouble with him is he is so large it's difficult to control him when he looses it' the officer said. 'He has absolutely no pain threshold.' I spoke to him briefly and he told me he was ok.

- - - - - - - -

Another prisoner who had been brought down to the Segregation unit after he had become very violent and cut his arms badly. They were heavily bandaged. When an officer opened the door he was standing on his bed trying to look out of the window. 'They've stolen my trainers' he told me almost hysterically. 'They are my trainers and I had to save for months to buy them. I am going to smash this place up until they give them to me back. You see that glass on the window? I am going to tear out every piece and cut myself in shreds.'

I suggested to the officer standing by me that I thought he should be in the healthcare unit rather than in the Seg. He told me that the unit was full and they would monitor him closely. I then asked the prisoner to tell me about his trainers and when he'd last seen them. He said they were worth 'at least' £80. He gave me a description and I said I would go to the wing, try to find out what happened to them and come back and tell him. 'You won't,' he said. 'They've really got it in for me here.'

It took a while to discover that they hadn't been stolen. When he cut himself his treasured trainers had been covered in blood. It made them a bio-hazard and a potential danger to both staff and prisoner. They had been placed in a protective covering and added to his property ready for when he was discharged. I went along to check and indeed they were there, but in a pretty bad state. I went back to tell him that I'd seen them and they would be waiting for him when he left the jail. He absorbed the information in a rather subdued way.

One young prisoner who had allegedly attacked an officer was angry that being in the Segregation Unit was stopping him working and earning some money to spend at the prison store. He handed me an application he had just written but had not yet been posted in the IMB box. Part of it read: 'My baby mother has just got her j'oyrow (Giro) and has only managed to send me £10 a week .' 'Baby mother' was a description I heard many times in prison and used by young men who seemed to want to distance themselves both from being an involved father and any financial responsibility for their child's upkeep. He looked to be in his early twenties and I asked him how many baby mothers he had. He thought carefully. 'Six' he said 'including this one, but I only see one.'

The mix of prisoners in the unit was always fascinating. One prisoner was dressed in a bright green and yellow onesie with a large E on the back, a hideous uniform designed especially to draw attention to those who might or had tried to escape. Wormwood Scrubs had a good intelligence system run by the Security Department. I was told they had heard that he was going to grab a set of keys from a female worker and then make a dash for it. He denied it. 'I would never do such a thing' he said self-righteously. 'Someone is telling porkies.'

Staff weren't taking any chances and he had been put in the Segregation Unit until he could be shipped out to another prison. Another young man in his early twenties had just been convicted of murder and was placed there for his own protection. An officer told me he'd heard there was a 'bounty' on his head. They would, he said, be transferring him to an 'A' category prison as soon as possible.

A third had refused to share a two-man cell. He claimed this was because he was HIV positive and had hepatitis and didn't want to give or get germs from this cell mate. Apparently the officer of the overcrowded wing asked him to share on a temporary basis until he could get someone from the healthcare unit to confirm his illnesses. They couldn't take what a prisoner said about his health at face value. The prisoner responded by throwing the sort of tantrum you see in two-year-olds when they don't get their own way and viciously attacked the prison officer. As a result, he was taken to the Segregation unit, where, ironically he would have a cell to himself.

Many of these hardened prisoners saw the independent monitors as a soft touch and a sympathetic ear, and often came up with sorrowful tales that sounded too awful to be true which they possibly were. One prisoner shed copious tears when I spoke to him claiming all he wanted was to see his little son who was 2½ years old, or at least be given some photographs of him. These he said were being kept along with the rest of his property elsewhere in the prison. Could I possibly arrange for them to be brought to his cell? Or better still go and get them. I checked with a member of staff and discovered he was facing several charges of indecency against small children and his photographs of a young child had been confiscated.

Another who had been sent to the Seg for breaking a television and disobeying an officer's order, told me he was suicidal and had tried to kill himself several times. 'I can't stay here,' he wailed. 'I cannot handle solitary confinement. I am going to start head-butting against the walls tomorrow unless I get returned to the wing. You had better tell everybody before I go further downhill.'

It was often difficult to know whether or not to believe such threats. Canny prisoners knew that threatening suicide could be useful as blackmail and would at the very least get them a lot of attention. It was equally true that a significant proportion of those who committed suicide in prison, a traumatising event that was officially called death in custody, took place in the Segregation Unit.

The correct thing to do was to tell a senior member of staff about any suicide threats. They knew the prisoner and could give a view on whether they thought he was telling the truth. Monitors could also authorise an Assessment, Care in Custody and Teamwork procedure, (ACCT), for prisoners we believed were at risk of self-harming or suicide. A special file would subsequently be opened and the individual officially be called a 'vulnerable prisoner'. He would then be closely monitored and a care plan would be prepared. Some prisoners hated this as they didn't like prison staff constantly checking on them. On one occasion eight out of the sixteen prisoners in the unit were on an ACCT. It was tough on the staff to monitor all of them very regularly.

While some prisoners recognized that I could help them and were extremely grateful, others, whose views of women veered to the Neanderthal, saw my visit as an opportunity to show how tough they were. I was warned about one prisoner who had a problem with women in authority. 'He is regularly down here for assaulting female officers' I was told. The prisoner was furious that the officer woke him up when he opened his cell door so I could talk to him. 'Why are you here?' he shouted at me. 'Leave me alone you useless fucking bitch.'

Another took offence at what I said. He had been moved to the Segregation unit for smashing up a television set in his cell and was feeling sorry for himself. 'I feel like a caged animal and am going fucking mad here,' he told me. 'I have to get out. I can't stand it without a television.' I suggested gently he should perhaps have thought about that before breaking his TV. He yelled expletives until the officer slammed the door shut.

Others expressed their displeasure at being disturbed even more unpleasantly. One prisoner was on his bed with his eyes closed when his cell door was opened. The officer introduced me and explained I was independent of the prison and I could help him with any problems he may have with regards to how he was being treated. He stared at me ominously as he hauled himself off the bed, then pulled down his prison-issued track bottoms to expose himself while moving like a seething panther towards the door. I shall never know whether this was an aggressive act towards me or that he needed the toilet that was situated behind the cell door as the officer by my side slammed the cell door shut. He asked me if I'd like to put in an official complaint. I said I'd think about it. This type of aggression made my heart beat faster and was a useful reminder how careful one should be.

– – – – – – – –

By far the most upsetting part of any visit was seeing how many seriously mentally ill and vulnerable men there were in the unit who desperately needed help. It was, for example, a salutary experience to see a grown man curled up in a foetal position on the floor in a corner of a cell who said nothing and barely moved. All one could do on these occasions was check from the door that he was breathing and press the point that he needed proper treatment and to be moved somewhere that could care for him more appropriately as soon as possible.

Another distressing case was a prisoner who had threatened to kill himself over an immigration issue. He was brought to the Segregations Unit because he was being violent. The officer said: 'He was only here ten minutes before he started bashing his head on the sink. Then he tried to suffocate himself with the mattress then kept taking a run at the door to bash his head again. I've called the doctor.'

It was obviously a loud cry for help. Another man told me he had been seen by the prison psychiatrist and that he had prescribed medication, but he didn't know what it was for or what the side effects could be. 'I tried to ask what is up with me and he couldn't answer,' he said. 'I get terrible psychological feelings in my head and I don't know what I am capable of. I have been coming in and out of here for the last four years and no one seems able to help me. ' Prisoners like him who might self-harm, were not allowed to keep a lighter or any sharp object in their cell. It was agony for this man to spend all day alone with his disturbing thoughts and the Government should be ashamed of how few specialist units exist for the mentally ill. If these were available the prison population would easily be halved.

Some prisoners just wanted to talk and if they preferred to do so in private and the officer believed I would be safe I used a small converted cell within the unit that had a table and two chairs. The routine was that I sat facing outwards, and the prisoner sat facing me with his back to the door, while a couple of officers quietly kept watch just outside. One older prisoner who wanted to talk to me - he was missing most of his teeth and looked at least sixty, but was apparently just over forty - was being discharged the following morning and was terrified. Someone had told him he could get help from the Citizens Advice Bureau, an organisation that he'd never heard of and that he could find the address from a library. I told him there were lots of CAB offices round London, including in the prison, which amazed him.

He wanted to go to King's Cross and I wrote down how to get there by underground, where the library was and who to ask for help. He had no idea how to use a computer but I re-assured him that library staff could look up the details he wanted. He was touchingly grateful. It was a small thing to do but left him feeling less anxious. The most difficult people to talk to were rapists although I rarely knew their crime until after I had seen them. It always surprised me that although I could never guess who was a murderer, I often sensed a rapist from their manner. They inevitably tried to undermine me, which was probably their default way of dealing with a female. One arrived in the small meeting room with about a dozen complaints he demanded I sort out. I suggested I dealt with three first, as there were lots of other prisoners who needed help that day.

It turned out he really wanted to hold forth. He used very long words when talking, occasionally incorrectly and insisted that everyone from the judge who ruled on his case to every officer on the wing was at fault, while he was always in the right. He claimed to be an expert in law, prison procedure, his human rights and the world at large. I am not a lawyer and my admission that I didn't know the specific law he quoted and would have to find out and get back to him gave him the opportunity he wanted. He started telling me how useless I was and asked why I bothered to come when I knew nothing. He was obviously hugely enjoying being insulting so I said he seemed clever enough to sort out his own problems, I said I had to go and told the officers hovering close by he could be locked up again. I later discovered he had raped several women. Paedophiles tended to behave entirely differently. They were usually older men who look like accountants or head teachers and were extremely polite. They inevitably said they were 'fine, thank you very much' and declined any help.

Ironically just as some prisoners begged me to help them get out of the unit, some prisoners, as extraordinary as may seem, were desperate to go to the Segregation Unit. They found it provided respite from a noisy wing, bullying and the stress of day to day prison life. One prisoner called it 'the best wing in the prison.' Some would even deliberately destroy their cell or get into a fight knowing the punishment would be time in the Segregation Unit where they would have 'a week or so of peace'. It could be so calming they would refuse to go back to the main wing. The governors did not want too many cells blocked in this way. It was important to keep cells available in case there was a disturbance but also vital for prisoners to mix with other prisoners and staff. The longer they stayed in solitary confinement the harder this became. Nor did it help them prepare for being released. Officers would try to persuade them to go back to their wing. If they really dug their heels in they risked being transferred to another jail.

-- -- -- -- --

There were usually between twelve and twenty five offenders in the Scrubs who were serving life sentences. The prison had little to offer them by way of facilities, courses or a sentence plan. They just had to wait, often in the Seg if they were dangerous, until a vacancy in a more suitable prison became available. This could take several months.

One lifer prisoner in the Seg refused to be transferred to a more suitable prison claiming it would fracture his relationship with his daughter. 'My relationship with her is the most important thing in my life,' he cried. 'If I am sent far away she will have trouble raising funds to come to see me. I must see her once a month. I won't get into the transfer van. I would rather die and she needs to see me as much as I need to see her. I won't let you jeopardise that.' He was one of countless others who failed to accept responsibility for the position he was in, wouldn't face reality and instead tried to blame everything on others. The officer with me explained patiently that it would affect his chance of parole hearing if he refused to go and a few days later four officers arrived to ensure one way or another he would get on the transfer van.

Occasionally a disgruntled prisoner would go on a hunger strike. This could be a way to make sure his grievances were listened to. Or an expression of deep-seated frustration with the prison system and/or himself. Every prisoner who refused food was carefully monitored and I talked to several over time. A common complaint was that they felt they had been singled out for bad treatment. I always tried to explain it was unlikely but that prison policy could give that impression. I also mentioned that there was virtually no chance they would be able to change anything by starving themselves as governors and politicians wouldn't give in to behaviour that could be interpreted as blackmail. The hunger strike rarely lasted more than a few days, but sometimes extended into weeks.

I visited the Unit at all times of the day and always found most of the prisoners, many of whom were in their twenties, laying in bed or sleeping. I never felt it was a productive way of dealing with these difficult and vulnerable men not least because it significantly diminished their ability to cope outside and that more creative thinking was needed.

Shortly after I arrived at the prison I asked if there were books available for prisoners in the Segregation Unit as they weren't allowed to go to the main prison library. I kept on asking and it was perhaps a triumph of sorts when, a couple of years later, a small open bookcase was placed in the Unit. It was something that may or may not have had anything to do with me. The few who could and wanted to read most enjoyed crime thrillers especially if they were violent, but at least it was better than staring at a blank wall. I also regularly asked the officers if they could have some A4 paper and a pencil so they could draw or write down their thoughts. The pencils were no bigger than my little finger and less of a potential weapon than one of normal size.

– – – – – – – –

Prisoners in the Unit were allowed a radio if their behaviour was not disruptive. They were not given a television despite the fact that the 2011 official government inspection of Wormwood Scrubs recommended that all prisoners in the Segregation Unit should be given TVs. The then senior Governor said he didn't approve of rewarding men who had been violent or disobedient with a television set especially if they had beaten up one of his officers and put him off duty for weeks. More recently there was the welcome development that one of the teachers from the education department within the prison came down to give any willing prisoner assignments to do in his cell.

The least civilised part of the Unit was the special accommodation cell. It has no window or chair, and there was usually a thin mattress on the ground instead of a bed. It was sometimes used for prisoners who had been very disruptive and they were put there for as little as fifteen minutes to cool down. Its most common use, however, was for prisoners on a dirty protest. This involved smearing themselves and the cell walls with excrement. This was not only a desperate protest but also another crude attempt at blackmail. Prisoners, and many were mentally unwell, often said they would stop if, for example, they were given a TV, extra tobacco or were sent to another prison. As with hunger strikes prisoners on a dirty protest couldn't be given in to and officers maintained the line they would only consider grievances once they stopped their protest.

A prisoner who started a dirty protest when on one of the wings could stay there if, once his action had been discovered, he immediately ended the protest. If he refused he was moved to the Segregation Unit. The prisoner was allowed to have some of his own possessions with him in the special accommodation cell but was warned that any property he couldn't properly clean afterwards would be destroyed. A CCTV camera hung from just below the ceiling to keep track of his movements. Sometimes prisoners managed to smear the camera with excrement so they couldn't be 'spied' on.

The independent monitors were always informed when a prisoner went on a dirty protest. Thick tape, a low screen and bio-hazard warnings were placed round the cell door and it was advisable not to get too close in case the prisoner had excrement he was waiting to throw at the next person he saw. I tried to visit the prisoner as soon as possible and developed a way of breathing through my mouth rather than my nose to limit the affects of the smell, but sometimes the stench was awful and I felt very sorry for the officers and other prisoners in the unit when this happened. It was not easy to make conversation with the prisoner, and, as many were naked I tried to keep my eyes focused on their face. Some sat with their back to the cell door and totally ignored me. Others talked or ranted. I managed to engage a few prisoners in conversation and successfully persuaded a couple to give up, have a shower and return to their cell. Often, to my disappointment I made no impression at all.

Some prisoners' views on their reasons for taking part in a dirty protest were incomprehensible. One prisoner told me he had less than six months of his sentence to run and had embarked on a dirty protest to show how fed up he was with prisons in general. 'I went down the shit process last week' he said. 'Prison is wearing me down. I will be using it now until I get out whenever something is unreasonable. Too many people are treating me like a tin of beans so I shall use shit on them.'

Like everything else in prison there was a strict protocol on how the situation had to be dealt with. If the prisoner was thought to be mentally ill, he would have a psychiatric assessment. He would also be seen daily by a doctor and a senior member of staff and every morning he would be asked if he wanted a shower and to end his protest.

The prisoner was also offered three meals a day. These were served with disposable cutlery and plates and he was given the chance to wash his hands before eating. The officer who had the unpleasant task of delivering the meal to the cell door would warn the prisoner in a loud voice as he approached that he had food for him, check if he wanted it, then open the door, place it just inside on the floor and relock the cell. Prison staff adopted a gentle, remarkably restrained approach to dirty protest prisoners, listened to whatever they wanted to say even when they shouted. The focus throughout was to end the protest. Most didn't last more than a few days but occasionally they lasted well over a month.

Certain prisoners were known to come off one dirty protest only to go back on it immediately they were placed back in a cell. This I was told was a ploy to try to contaminate as many cells as possible and effectively close down the Unit. Serious efforts were made by staff to stop this happening and the bio-hazard team of volunteer prisoners were brought in to make sure the cells were cleaned and back in action as soon as possible. It was an unenviable task for which they were paid little more than £1 a session.

CHAPTER SIX
JUDGMENT DAYS

Those who breached prison discipline rules were required to appear at an adjudication hearing held in a small side room in the Segregation Unit. It was the prison's version of a court and usually overseen by prison staff, usually governors. An independent adjudicator, who was either a district judge or a magistrate, came about once a month to hear more serious cases.

An established level of discipline is essential for the effective running of any prison and about 100,000 prisoners a year from prisons round the country break prison rules. These rules included failing a mandatory drug test, obstructing an officer in his line of duty, disobeying an order, or being in possession of an illicit article or substance, assaulting an officer or another prisoner.

Erring prisoners had to be given the relevant paperwork, commonly known as a 'nicking sheet', within two days of the alleged wrongdoing. At the start of any hearing they had to be asked if they understood what was happening, if they had had enough time to think about what it was alleged they had done, if they had written anything down they would like to submit, which was very rare, if they wanted a solicitor and if they were pleading guilty or not guilty. At one hearing I attended, even the decision of whether or not to plead guilty was too much for one prisoner, who replied: 'A bit of each.'

The prison officer involved at the time an offence was committed was also required to be present to give evidence. The prisoner had his say, a witness, usually a fellow prisoner, was heard and the officer would then briefly comment on the prisoner's behaviour, and whether or not he complied with the prison regime. If a lawyer was present he could cross-examine the officer and any witness.

Independent monitors were encouraged to attend these adjudications to observe that the process was fair. It was always an absorbing experience but sometimes, if there were disturbed prisoners in the Segregation Unit deliberately making a noise while the adjudication was in progress, it was difficult to hear what was going on. On one occasion three disturbed prisoners banged on their cell doors and constantly rang the emergency cell bell for at least an hour. It gave me a headache but the officers running the hearing carried on as if nothing had happened.

The independent adjudicator could add up to 42 days to a prisoner's sentence, but governors' punishments were mainly restrictive: stopping prisoners mixing socially, getting paid for any work they were doing within the prison and not letting them buy extra food and/or toiletries. The ban usually lasted about two weeks

Prisoners on these internal charges were brought to the Seg from other wings by an officer and kept in a cell until it was their turn to be heard. They then sat at the end of a table opposite the adjudicator with one, two or three prison officers close by depending on how volatile they were judged to be. Some were polite and referred to the adjudicator as 'Sir.' Others struggled to understand the simplest explanations. All the governors and independent adjudicators I listened to over a number of years bent over backwards to be fair to the prisoner, explained processes carefully and overall gave the impression that they would really rather not punish them if they would only try that bit harder to behave.

This was particularly apparent when one obviously educated prisoner appeared. The independent adjudicator told him he was sympathetic to his plight. 'Things just haven't been going your way,' he said. 'You are obviously an intelligent young man but I have to add 20 days to your sentence. If you behave yourself for six months and have no more adjudications you can make an appeal to the governor and he can take half it.'

On the other hand many prisoners played the system masterfully. The procedures were easily manipulated and if a prisoner's release date was coming up he could drag out the process so that it couldn't be completed by the time he was released, at which point any charges were dropped. Adjudicators knew this but couldn't do anything about it.

- - - - - - - -

The most common offence that came before the judge or magistrate was being in possession of a mobile phone. Mobiles give prisoners the opportunity to order drugs, intimidate witnesses and continue their criminal lives. Despite the banning, prisons round the country are awash with both mobiles and SIM cards. Wormwood Scrubs is no exception. Mobiles were thrown over the prison wall, smuggled in during visiting times, and very occasionally brought in by a member of staff who could be seduced by the amount of money to be made. The going rate in prison for a mobile was £300-£500, while Sim cards sold for £20. Mobile phone jamming devices are available but present legal and technical challenges as they cannot be allowed to affect phones outside the prison perimeter. This is particularly valid for Wormwood Scrubs as there is a hospital close by.

About 200 mobiles were found each year during the cell and body searches that are a regular part of prison life. Others remained undiscovered. Many prisoners hid mobiles up their rectum. Other hiding places included tied behind a prisoner's testicles and stuffed in a box of cereal.

While it was impossible for a prisoner to deny he had a mobile when it had been secreted on his body, he usually did when it was found in his cell. Excuses were often creative but seasoned officers had heard them all before. For example one prisoner claimed that when his cellmate was released he gave him his unfinished box of Sugar Puffs cereal and he had no idea there was a mobile inside. Another said he found a mobile in the shower, brought it back to the cell with the intention of handing it over to an officer but then forgot all about it. A third said a violent prisoner bullied him into looking after it for him and that he had never used it. All three of these prisoners were found guilty of the offence. At one adjudication the prisoner refused to plead despite the officer stating that the mobile fell out of his tracksuit bottoms while he was in the cell. The officer explained: 'During a cell search the prisoner was seen trying to hide something in his trousers. I gave him instructions to move his hands away from his tracksuit but he refused to comply. Shortly afterwards the phone dropped on the floor.'

The prisoner disagreed with the officer's version of events. His version was that five officers came to the cell to search it and told him to strip. 'I refused. I have serious personal problems stripping with people around me,' he explained. He added that the officers then took him to a 'holding room' where prisoners were kept if they were en route to different wings and asked him 'aggressively' to strip. It was so cold in the room he said he didn't want to. The adjudicator was sympathetic to the prisoner's discomfort at being 'strip-searched in front of too many people' and asked him if he'd like to defer the case and talk to a solicitor. He said he didn't. 'I just want to get it over and done with.' The adjudicator was told the prisoner was violent and a troublemaker and had attended five adjudications over the last few months for refusing to be transferred to another prison. The adjudication was postponed so that the prison could prepare a management plan for him.

A stomach-churning adjudication involved an officer who found a prisoner in the process of trying to push a mobile up his rectum. He added: 'I managed to stop him and retrieve it after a brief struggle.' Working in a prison is not for the faint-hearted.

Being present at adjudications provided an extraordinary glimpse into the way many prisoners think. Although it is wise not to generalise, I observed certain similarities time and time again. Most of them were incredibly immature, particularly if they were serial criminals. If they had spent time in a Young Offenders Unit and subsequently an adult prison their experience of the world was very narrow and they had little experience in negotiating or verbally managing difficult situations. Instead their default way of dealing with an accusation was to shout threats or become violent. It didn't help that their upbringing, or lack or it, left them with little clue of what was right and wrong and they saw everything from their own very narrow subjective point of view. They didn't seem able to understand that their actions had consequences.

A large number were also paranoid. Time and time again prisoners would say to me: 'They (prison officers) are out to get me.' They seemed to believe that the vast prison was run deliberately to 'wind me up' and overreacted when something didn't go their way. They lacked a sense of proportion and could be their own worst enemies. One prisoner who was in trouble for smashing up his cell and causing hundreds of pounds worth of damage offered the following explanation. 'I am always unlocked last to get food. It's deliberate. So I smashed the sink in my cell. The screws took away my TV and left me without a sink for a week. It's my human right to have running water. It's why I went on a hunger strike. The screws are playing games with me. If they want to be hostile I'll be hostile back. In any case, after three days you stop being hungry and just get headaches.' Adopting a tit-for-tat approach was ill-advised. A young prisoner told me: 'The screws are being awkward with me so I am being awkward with them. One of them started winding me up so I hit him.' He had several days added to his sentence.

- - - - - - - -

Many prisoners fall back on the Human Rights Act when things don't go their own way. One prisoner accused of slamming an officer's hand in his cell door, causing a broken bone and a badly damaged ligament, was unrepentant. The injury was so serious that senior staff debated whether to hand the prisoner over to the police, and potentially a substantial new sentence, or put him before the independent adjudicator, where he was likely to have only a few days added to his prison term. The latter option was chosen. The prisoner justified himself to the adjudicator by saying: 'The screw came into my cell and I wanted him to leave because I needed to go to the toilet.' He was asked why he didn't explain this to the officer. 'I can't get involved in that,' he replied dismissively. 'Coming in at that time was a breach of my human rights.'

Another prisoner was furious that the adjudicator stated he intended to stop him buying extra food supplies for two weeks as a punishment for continually disobeying an officer's order. Barely concealing his anger, he said: 'It is coming up to Christmas and if you don't let me have canteen (the name for the prison shop) I am sure it is a breach of my human rights.' Surprisingly, the adjudicator softened and told him how to appeal against the punishment.

One prisoner with a reputation for violence was particularly menacing telling the presiding magistrate he would not go to a normal wing and quoted his legal rights. The magistrate told him not to tell him how to do his job, but remanded him back into the Segregation Unit. One officer was disappointed. 'We want to get him moved to another prison but if he spends all his time in the Seg, no other prison will take him, because they will know just how difficult he is' I was told. 'We want to swap him for another prisoner who might be even worse but at least it will be a change.'

Some prisoners refused to believe that they couldn't call some or all the shots in prison. One man with the habit of saying "innit" at the end of almost every sentence had recently been brought back to prison for breaking the terms of his early release. He was full of self-righteous indignation when he appeared at an adjudication for disobeying an order. 'They wanted to put someone in my cell and I was not going to have that, innit,' he began. 'I don't want to share the cell with someone I don't know because I might have had history with them, innit. Officers dragged me down to the floor. I couldn't stand up. They then gave me a nicking.' The officer said he had threatened violence. 'No,' he insisted. 'I just refused to let someone in my cell.'

Prisoners who had problems with women in authority or thought of them in very crude terms were regularly in trouble. One young female officer complained about a prisoner who, she alleged, had brushed too closely past her and grabbed her shoulders. She added that he had had plenty of space to pass her on the stairway of one of the wing landings without touching her. The prisoner pleaded not guilty, denied there was enough room to pass without brushing past her and claimed that touching her had been an accident and that he had said, 'Shit, sorry.'

The officer admitted she had not been hurt and if that had been the only problem with the prisoner she might well have just given him a verbal warning. But when she told him his behaviour was unacceptable he lost his temper and allegedly shouted 'I wouldn't touch you, you dirty bitch' and threatened to 'wreck' her face. This prisoner was, however, known for being volatile and it brought up a tricky dilemma. Should all prisoners be treated the same? Or should allowances be made for those who have personality issues? Another female officer might have ignored the way he brushed past her, especially as she hadn't been hurt. She might have viewed what was alleged to have happened as a sign of the prisoner's immaturity rather than an assault. But the female officer in question felt the prisoner knew exactly what he was doing and shouldn't be allowed to get away with it. He was found guilty and sent to a cell in the Seg. He immediately began banging on the cell door and soon afterwards went on a dirty protest. Turning a blind eye might have avoided his volcanic response, but it might also have left the officer open to increasing harassment.

Another incident brought before the adjudicator was far more unpleasant. A prisoner rang his bell early one evening. The female officer asked him through the cell door what he wanted. He replied, 'an envelope.' She subsequently opened the observation panel on the cell door to let him know he would have to wait until the following morning. She saw that he was lying on the bed holding his erect penis in his hands and staring intensely at her. The adjudicator was told the prisoner had immigration problems, was a drug addict and 'not 100 per cent.' When he was asked if he had anything to say, the prisoner mumbled, 'I didn't mean no harm.' Twelve days were added to his sentence with the offer that if he behaved himself for six months, he could ask for the extra sentence to be reduced by half.

■ ■ ■ ■ ■ ■ ■ ■

Assaults against fellow prisoners and staff was the default way many prisoners expressed their frustrations. One prisoner charged with wounding his cellmate pleaded guilty but in mitigation claimed he was trying to keep himself out of trouble. 'I just want to get on with my sentence even though people have been annoying me,' he said. He added that his cellmate had threatened him continually including telling him he would be murdered. 'I lost my temper and hit him in the face,' he said. He was given fourteen extra days on his sentence.

Another assault followed the recent installation of an all-weather football pitch that cost £57,000. Two prisoners argued over a casual match between inmates and one punched the other before the fracas was brought under control. Both men were brought before the adjudicator. The injury was 'a nick on the lip' and hadn't required treatment. The case for assault was proven but the perpetrator, who was in prison for the first time, and was described as 'polite with OK behaviour' was due to be released in a few weeks. The adjudicator told him it was clearly not acceptable that he had assaulted another prisoner for getting on his nerves but as the injury was minor his punishment would only be 14 days' loss of earnings and 14 days' loss of canteen.

Serious assaults on prison officers were equally common. The difference was that prison officers had to be particularly careful how they reacted when trying to protect themselves. There were strict and specific procedures on how prisoners could be restrained and officers could be in serious trouble for using what could be described as too much force.

Adjudications also covered the possession of illegal drugs and failing a drug test. The latter was commonly known as 'the piss test'. I cover the subject of drugs more fully in another chapter but regular drug users who were nearing the end of their sentence were expert at getting round charges relating to the test. If they were found guilty they asked for an adjournment, then for time to find a solicitor and then for an independent analysis of the sample. There was nothing the adjudicator could do. 'It takes three weeks for an independent sample to be analysed,' he said. 'This often takes the prisoner to the end of his sentence and he gets off.' Other prisoners pleaded to be given a second chance. One claimed he was on drugs only for the week he was tested. 'I've since been trying to get my head straight, sir,' he pleaded. 'I plan to start anew when I get out.' The external adjudicator gave no indication about whether he had heard this excuse countless times before and told him he would give him a chance. He added eighteen days to the length of his sentence but suspended them for six months, adding: 'If there are no further slip-ups the eighteen days will disappear.' Pleading for a second chance, however, didn't work for another prisoner who had previously failed the drug test on nine occasions.

Inevitably there were discrepancies between how a prison officer and a prisoner recalled an incident and I never attended an adjudication when the prisoner was believed rather than the officer. If proving the case rested on believing one or the other, the officer always won. Sometimes adjudicators were surprisingly lenient. One prisoner was charged with being in possession of hooch, which is prison alcohol made out of warm water, orange juice, bread and sugar. The prisoner pleaded that he was 'in the wrong place at the wrong time. I was ordered by another prisoner to hold a container of hooch for him for a few weeks. I panicked and did what I was told.' The adjudicator responded to his 'unusual circumstances' and added four days to his sentence suspended for six months that could be cancelled if he behaved himself.

Prison officers kept a sharp eye out for oranges in a prisoner's cell, especially if they were beginning to ferment as it was a sign the oranges could be used to make alcohol. I was reminded of this when a prisoner approached me saying he was unwell and suffering from a poor diet: could I please arrange for him to be provided with several oranges each day? I suggested politely that it would be best if he first saw the doctor.

-- -- -- -- -- --

The adjudications' room was also used for senior staff to review offenders in the Segregation Unit and decide what to do with them next and how to get them back on a normal wing. Monitors, the individual prisoner, officers and a healthcare representative were expected to attend. I remember one detainee who categorically refused to leave the Segregation Unit. 'It will be a joke, man,' he said when the adjudicator told him he had to return to a wing. 'This place is a shithole and it wouldn't happen in any other prison to be sent to a wing where you don't want to be. I didn't come into this room to be told 'no'. You have no idea how violent I can be even if there is a restraint on me.' It was a tricky one. The usual punishment for disobeying an order is a spell in the Segregation Unit. This, of course, was precisely what the prisoner wanted. The adjudicator gave him seven more days in the Seg but warned him that would be that. I don't know the outcome but in cases like this the prisoner is often moved to another jail, by force if necessary.

A remand prisoner also refused to relocate to a wing because of a rape he had served a sentence for some years previously. The adjudicator was unsympathetic. 'You are not currently being charged with an offence of a sexual nature,' he said. 'We have lots of people on the mainstream wings who have been charged with rape. You just need to keep your head down. You will have good support there and it is far better for your mental health to be around other people.' The prisoner replied that he felt he was tainted for life, was depressed and couldn't cope with the move at the present time. The adjudicator told him that he would let him stay in the Segregation Unit for one more week and suggested he use the time to build up his mental health. The prisoner then asked to see a psychiatrist. The adjudicator said he could certainly see a doctor but added this warning: 'There is healthcare available to you but there are over 1,200 inmates in this prison, many of whom have far more serious psychiatric problems.'

Vulnerable prisoners who had been given an ACCT, (Assessment, Care in Custody and Teamwork) were also seen within the Segregation Unit. They had been put under close supervision because they were likely to self-harm. ACCT reviews regularly re-assessed these prisoners and involved a governor, a nurse from healthcare, a senior officer and, if possible, an independent monitor. The prisoner was also invited to be party to the discussion. Copious and detailed notes were taken throughout, as the decision to close an ACCT, which meant the prisoner would no longer be closely monitored, was always difficult because a wrong decision could have fatal consequences. The governor explained the process of the review to the prisoner, asked him how he was and if he was likely to self-harm or kill himself. Prisoners were asked the same question in Reception when they arrived in the jail and I always wondered if someone intent on taking his own life would admit it in such a public way.

One vulnerable young prisoner on an ACCT also had a long list of wrongdoing to his name. This included insulting a female officer and refusing to give a urine sample for a drug test.

He seemed to show no fear and despite his age behaved like someone who held all the cards. It might have been bravado to cover up his nerves but he gave every impression that he didn't care and tried to banter with the governor, which was totally inappropriate. For example, when he was asked to give a urine sample, he replied he would only think about it if the governor first gave him some cigarettes as he had run out of tobacco. The governor told him rather kindly that trying to manipulate or bribe him wouldn't work. 'Sorry, mate,' the prisoner replied, 'then I ain't doing nothing.'

It is a stipulation when reviewing an ACCT that the governor made 'every effort' to engage with the prisoner. But it was impossible to engage with someone who was obviously not interested in compromise or obeying a prison order. The governor did his best. He told him that if he gave a sample, he would think about getting him some tobacco. The prisoner replied: 'it has to be the other way round.' He added 'I don't trust nobody. First you have to show me respect and loyalty, because that is what I expect, and then I'll think about a sample.' It is a dilemma for senior staff to know how to deal with this new breed of young criminals who appear to have no conscience, self-awareness, fear or respect and would view any soft prison policy with derision.

The governor moved on to talk about the ACCT. He asked again if he was likely to harm himself and received a negative answer. The prisoner went back to his cell and the governor asked the senior officer, the nurse and myself if we thought he should close the ACCT. I was particularly interested in the view of the nurse but she said she didn't know the prisoner and opted out. I wondered why she hadn't studied his notes or asked a colleague before coming down to the Segregation Unit. After some discussion the ACCT was closed.

A second ACCT review had a more positive feel. The young prisoner bounced into the room full of smiles. When asked how he was he replied, 'I feel strong and healthy. I am keeping myself fit and my mind occupied.' It was so obviously the right thing to say I wondered if he had learnt it by heart. He added how much his medication had helped and he how he had turned over a new leaf. He agreed he had been brought down to the Segregation Unit because he had smashed up his cell on another wing and that he had been violent and threatened suicide.

But he said that although it was only a few days ago it seemed a long way away. He was asked if he really thought he wouldn't self-harm again. 'That's all in the past,' he smiled. 'While you have been down here in the Segregation Unit you have behaved well and been a very nice man,' the governor enthused. 'It's just that you don't seem to do well on a wing.'

'I am going to work hard to get a job on the wing,' he replied, 'and focus on that.' He had prepared himself well and the ACCT was closed. The senior officer took me to one side. 'He responds well in the Seg because he likes the discipline and restrictions,' he said. 'I have no idea how he will be when he goes back on a wing. He finds it extremely difficult to cope.'

CHAPTER SEVEN
SELF HARM AND SUICIDE

I t was a daily challenge for many prisoners to stay clear of the tough inmates on their wing. Despite the prison's mission statement that there is 'no tolerance' of bullies this wasn't a deterrent in itself. Life on the wings could be intimidating, confusing and noisy, and sometimes the atmosphere made prisoners fearful for their lives. Bullies, drug dealers and champion manipulators could seem to be everywhere. There were also 'snitchers' who acted as spies and passed on information to staff that could be valuable. The security system and intelligence network at the Scrubs was the pride of the prison and its tentacles reached far and wide. A prisoner in the Segregation Unit told me he had given officers lots of information and had been put there for his own protection as he thought he had been discovered and was waiting to be transferred to another jail. I never found out if it was true.

Street gangs have turned juvenile prisons into dangerous war zones but not yet made an equivalent impact on adult jails. Feltham Prison for young offenders in Middlesex has identified 147 different gangs. Many inmates lived in fear of their lives and one young prisoner was brutally attacked by a mob of ten who stamped on his head and nearly killed him. From November 2013 this became a potential problem for the Scrubs.

A year or so before there had been signs that adult gang culture was becoming an increasing problem. Some senior staff showed their irritation when the word 'gang' was mentioned and told monitors not to use the 'emotive' word. Instead they insisted that in Wormwood Scrubs they were 'groups' rather than 'gangs' and that nationalities like Somalis, Pakistanis or Poles 'bonded together' for protection and company. The staff on the wings had either not been told of this stipulation or took no notice as nearly every month the wing reports included items on 'gang' activity. It was hard not to feel that we were being somewhat manipulated.

Certainly the fluidity of the prison population meant that alliances were often ephemeral. If governors heard about a gang building up, they moved obvious members to another wing, with next to no notice. Sometimes all that was left of the friendship would be occasional shouts through the cell windows.

Alternatively one or two gang members would be transferred to other prisons. Selected staff would be informed well in advance, but it was important to keep the prisoner in the dark in case he reacted violently to the idea. Instead, he was given just enough time to pack his things. It made sense as prisoners could react violently. One hurled himself from a wing landing, an action that was noted as a suicide attempt. Another climbed on to the netting of a landing and refused to leave it until he was assured that he would stay in Wormwood Scrubs. He was talked down after several hours by experienced prison negotiators who did not promise him anything.

Coping with the daily slots of socialising on the wing wasn't easy for all but the most confident prisoners and trust between inmates was a rare commodity. One prisoner who enjoyed playing pool told me he would never play in prison because he wouldn't know if the prisoner he played with could turn violent if he lost. Prisoners who found it difficult to mix or were new to the wing often stood on their own with their backs to the wall looking as terrified as rabbits caught in headlights. Unfortunately for them their anxiety sent out a signal that they were ripe for bullying to those prisoners who were on the look out for someone to control, run errands and/or store illicit goods on their behalf.

By contrast some inmates felt more at home in prison than they did on the outside. One prisoner who complained to me about the way Wormwood Scrubs was being run was keen to impress with his expertise on the matter. 'Look,' he began proudly. 'I know what I'm talking about. I have been in countless prisons up and down the country. Those in London include Pentonville, Wandsworth and Belmarsh and I am telling you this one is the worst of the lot.' Many others shared his TripAdvisor mentality and would point out in particular that 'the health care is shit and so is the food.'

- - - - - - - -

Although Wormwood Scrubs was a local prison where many inmates did not stay for long I saw the same faces come back time and again. Nearly 60% of prisoners serving a sentence of less than 12 months reoffend within a year and 47% of adults are reconvicted within one year of release. When in the jail they would tell me how pleased they were that they were halfway through their sentence and would soon be released. 'This time I'm not coming back,' they would declare. Months later they would return. One long-serving prison officer said he saw the same faces repeatedly over a 25-year period. It was immensely sad.

One chatty prisoner, who had lost most of his teeth, was pleased to be back in the Scrubs and away from the cold and wet. 'I'm 56 now,' he explained, 'and I've been in and out of here since I was in my early twenties. All I know is how to burgle. Not that I hurt anyone, mind. How do they expect me to do anything else? At least it's warm and I'm fed and don't have bills to worry about.' Another was desperate to change his life. 'I'm going to be forty next year, Miss' he began. 'I've got to do something to stop coming in here. I want to turn over a new leaf and get a job, be responsible. Any ideas?' We talked a little. He said his mother had thrown him out of the house when he was eleven as her then new boyfriend didn't like him. He fended for himself largely on the street, didn't go to school but avoided drugs. He told me he liked to write and showed me some of his work. It was based on his life and while the spelling was phonetic and the grammar quite rough it was moving and compelling. It was salutary to feel that if he had been born into a supportive family his life might have taken quite a different route.

Some prisoners with sentences of between three months and four years were allowed out on a scheme called Home Detention Curfew or Electronic Tagging. The prisoner was released early and fitted with an electronic tag around his ankle. In exchange he had to stay at a chosen and approved address for 12 hours – usually overnight – and allow a machine to be set up to verify the 12-hour curfew. If he didn't abide by the curfew he would be returned to jail. Those I spoke to on their return to prison rarely admitted any slip-ups had been their fault. 'I refused to go into the hostel I was supposed to go into because it was full of junkies and they recalled me because of that,' said one disparagingly. 'Now the governor says I have to serve my full sentence of three years for armed robbery. It's not fair but I am trying to rehabilitate myself with my mind. I read books, don't watch television and officers tell me I am a quiet, pleasant person. '

One self-righteous prisoner complained both about being brought back to prison and that he was put onto a basic regime. 'They said I breached my sex offenders' register but all I did was go into a garden,' he said. 'When I was arrested I demanded to be taken to another prison because it has better facilities and instead I was brought here. Since then I have lost all my privileges. I suffer from severe anxiety and need a radio and TV to keep me going. I am being punished by spending 24 hours a day in a cell in silence. This place is like Colditz. I want to be transferred out of here as soon as possible.'

A high percentage of problems in the prison was caused by very few prisoners. Research by the Psychology Department at Wormwood Scrubs in 2006 found that fewer than ten individuals were responsible for more than 50% of incidents of difficult or disruptive behaviour. Very difficult prisoners were usually mentally ill, hard-core prisoners, or had previously been in a young offenders' prison and had no realistic means of accessing a different life. Excluding the mentally ill, the two other types were deeply cynical, focused on themselves and had tunnel vision. Their childhoods were classically dysfunctional. Many had been born to young single mothers who were often addicts, and they had been abused or neglected as children. There was no male role model in their lives, they had truanted at school and were basically left to bring themselves up. They were obviously damaged, over-reacted to the smallest thing and responded to anything they didn't like with violence rather than words.

– – – – – – – –

Managing prisoners with complex behaviour issues could be extremely stressful for staff and other prisoners. They took up a lot of officers' time, and could be very disruptive in a wing, smashing, flooding or setting fire to their cells, perhaps in a desperate attempt to get some of the attention they missed out on as children. They were in and out of the Segregation Unit, where they regularly went on dirty protests. At one point a part of one wing was allocated to provide a special unit for these difficult men with a full staff allocation to give them more attention in an attempt to reduce their violent behaviour. The staff in this unit were extraordinary.

It takes a special sort of officer who doesn't always need to pull rank and lets the prisoner get away with more than he would ordinarily because of his chronic personality issues. These men are the tragic walking wounded in our society and so chronically damaged that the public must be protected from them, but it is shocking that so little is done to help them tackle their issues.

One of the 'difficult' men was intelligent, sharp-witted and when he was having a good day had a certain charm. I saw him on one occasion when he had just been told the staff were fed up with him. He said rather sadly in a moment of self-introspection: 'I know they are trying to get rid of me. They say I am a liar and a cheat, but I don't think I am the worst prisoner in the world. I want to stay here. I don't like being with new people. Do you think I could get some sort of job in the prison?' I said he might be able to if he let himself take orders and did what he was told which he far too often refused to do.

He was, however, very impulsive, had an incredibly short fuse and no proper idea of what was and wasn't appropriate behaviour. He smashed up his cell so many times he must have cost the prison a fortune. He was also self-destructive and ruined every chance he was given. For example, when the prisoner was in the Segregation Unit waiting to attend an adjudication for disobeying an order and the officer went to collect him he told the officer he wasn't ready as he wanted to clean his teeth properly before he attended the session. The independent adjudicator, a district judge, patiently waited quite a time for him, but as he had a busy list, found the case against him proved and had the next prisoner brought in.

When the prisoner was told what had happened he started banging endlessly on his cell door. Yet he had brought it entirely on himself. I often saw him in the Seg and he seemed to have no idea how to have a straightforward relationship with either staff or other prisoners. It was unclear whether he was suffering from a personality disorder, had a mental illness, or his behaviour was the result of an abusive childhood. One officer said he wasn't mad, just bad and it would take many years of intense therapy to bring him round. He improved in the special unit, at least for a while and was given a job washing the wing floors. 'Miss, miss,' he called out one day when I was passing. 'See, I've got a job and I'm doing what I'm told.' He was triumphant. It didn't last. He was released a few weeks later but was back in the Scrubs again after about a month looking sadder and more defeated.

Another prisoner placed in the special unit was hard, tough and prone to attacks of violence. He too was in and out of the Segregation Unit but never exercised with other prisoners because of his unpredictable violence. He bore grudges and was vengeful and officers dealt with him carefully. He often seemed like a grumbling volcano waiting to erupt. He didn't stay long in the unit before he was swapped for another 'difficult' prisoner from another jail.

A third prisoner was relentlessly disruptive and I was present in the wing unit when an officer tried to give him a helpful, almost paternal, talking-to. 'You have a very childish attitude,' he began. 'You need to start taking responsibility for what has happened to you and then change it. You must try to behave yourself or things will go from bad to worse. If you do that you will be able to come off the basic regime and even get a television in your cell. I am one of the most tolerant people in the jail but even I cannot always cope with you.' After the conversation, the officer took me aside. 'I think he had an abusive father. If we stand up to him he bolts like a scared rabbit to the back of the cell. People think all we do is bang people up but we do actually try to help them.' Officers like him were remarkable individuals.

A special case study was done of each of these prisoners that highlighted the issues that could trigger violence. Although attempts were made to help the men change their behaviour and not automatically resort to acts of violence, there was no quick fix. Officers who dealt with them were advised to go easy and avoid deliberately winding them up or escalating a situation. This worked while the prisoners were in the special unit, but the unit was abandoned because of cost-cutting a few years later.

– – – – – – – –

At the other end of the scale were those prisoners who kept silent and caused no trouble at all. They were the forgotten ones who withdrew from the regime, did not mix with other prisoners and spent the maximum time they could in their cell. They were often at risk of self-harming and suicide.

One of the key duties of the Prison Service is to keep prisoners 'in safe custody'. Dealing with prisoners who were at risk of harming themselves or others was the responsibility of the Safer Custody Department. It was an area of increasing responsibility. The Howard League for Penal Reform, the world's oldest penal reform charity, called for urgent action after figures for 2013 showed that there had been a sharp increase in the number of self-inflicted deaths behind bars. Five of these deaths were recorded at Wormwood Scrubs, the highest amongst all prisons in England and Wales. The League also voiced particular concern over suicide among young offenders in adult prisons. According to Ministry of Justice statistics, 198 deaths were reported in jails during 2013. Of these, about 70 were self-inflicted, the highest rate in six years and about 100 prisoners died of natural causes. There were also four alleged murders. The charity stated it believed the increased figures were a result of cuts to prison regimes and budgets. In one sample month, September 2011 The Offender Health Performance Report revealed that in Wormwood Scrubs there were nine incidents of self harm. Four of the incidents were attempted hangings, two were lacerations, one was an attempted self-strangulation, one was an overdose and one was the result of a prisoner jumping from one high landing to the one below.

The Safer Custody unit at Wormwood Scrubs followed specific procedures to keep prisoners safe. Concerns about prisoners came to their attention in a variety of ways. If an officer, nurse, doctor or monitor thought a prisoner was depressed or suicidal he or she could put him on an Assessment, Care in Custody and Teamwork (ACCT). A specific folder was then opened that went with the prisoner wherever he was in the jail and staff were supposed to write comments about his condition and behaviour. One of the purposes of an ACCT was to find out the key issues that made a prisoner anxious and how they could be avoided. Instructions on how this must be done were contained in a dense 70-page document that covered every possible scenario including who should be involved in administering and supervising the ACCT, how often it should be reviewed and the number of times the prisoner should be observed, both per day and per hour. Prisoners on ACCTs were encouraged to attend discussions about themselves. Some refused to engage, others enjoyed the attention and sometimes played up.

Although it is a worthy document realistically it is impossible to accurately predict whether someone is going to harm himself or, worse, commit suicide. Managing an ACCT was also so time-consuming for staff that the paperwork was not always kept up to scratch. Nor were some officers keen on the detailed procedure. 'It is important for an officer to make sure he knows his prisoners and keep an eye on them,' said one. 'But the powers that be make it increasingly difficult. Nowadays if a prisoner says he is suicidal an ACCT is opened so the custody department can cover its back and if a prisoner commits suicide, the member of staff who happened to be on duty at the time is blamed.'

Sometimes an officer asked me to speak to a prisoner or detainee he was worried about, and sometimes monitors tried to see everyone who was on an ACCT on a wing. But it was rather random and those really at risk might not be noticed. When I first arrived at the prison I was shocked to see male prisoners walking around the wings with slashed arms. I subsequently came across much worse. I heard about and spoke to prisoners who, as well as slashing themselves, tried to eat light bulbs, wire, and even ripped-up flooring. According to Ministry of Justice statistics, younger prisoners tended to self-harm and be involved in assault incidents more often than older prisoners, while suicide rates among prisoners tended to peak among those in their thirties.

There was help available. Prisoners had access to Listeners, a peer support effort where prisoners were trained and backed up by Samaritans to listen in complete confidence to the anxieties and distress of fellow prisoners 24-hours a day. The objectives were to assist in reducing the number of self-inflicted deaths, reduce self-harm and help those in distress. It started in 1991, now has more than 1,200 active Listeners and is available in nearly every prison in the country. Every prisoner who volunteered was first cleared by the prison's security team and then put on an intensive course based on the Samaritans training but adapted for use in a prison. Listeners did not receive any remuneration for their work.

The numbers of Listeners at the Scrubs fluctuated. In the mid 2000s its activities stopped altogether because one branch of the Samaritans could no longer support it. It took a while to get going again with another branch. At the last count there were about 14 Listeners in the Scrubs. It was a terrific idea but in practice prisoners didn't use them much, perhaps because they found it so difficult to trust anyone. The other negative issue was the rapid turnover of inmates at the jail. Prisoners wouldn't be offered training unless they were likely to stay put for more than six months, partly because the Samaritans didn't have the resources to run many training programmes. The pool for potential Listeners was often confined to remand prisoners or detainees waiting to be deported.

Prisoners could also call the Samaritans direct via a dedicated phone line that was free and confidential. I remember a prisoner in the Segregation Unit who insisted on calling the Samaritans several times at night and spoke for long periods of time. The phone was finally removed. Distressed prisoners could also talk to a member of the Chaplaincy.

- - - - - - - -

A death in custody, whether by natural causes or self-inflicted, was always traumatic for a prisoner's family, his cellmates and the duty officers. I know of several occasions when staff saved a prisoner's life by acting quickly and expertly but they couldn't always be successful. Following a death there were strict procedures to adhere to. Every death in custody had to be reported promptly to a variety of people including the police, the prisoner's next of kin, the coroner, senior officials in the Prison Service and the independent monitors.

During my three years as Chair of the Wormwood Scrubs IMB, staff always tried to get hold of me first. It was common practice to go in as soon as possible to find out how and where the prisoner was found, and talk to any members of staff who were involved. A 'hot debrief' took place as soon as possible to gather details of the incident and there was a subsequent debrief at a later date. The Prison Governor was required to write a letter of condolence to the family. He also had to offer to contribute towards the funeral expenses and invite the late prisoner's family to visit the prison. Families often took up this offer, which was traumatic for them and staff.

Officers who were involved when the body was found or who had tried to save the prisoner's life were allowed to go home. Some found the experience so traumatising they took sick leave for several weeks. Others preferred to stay at their post. One young officer who had witnessed a death earlier in the day told me how traumatising it had been but that he decided to stay at work. 'A few of the officers went home' he said, 'but the wing was so short staffed I thought it was important to stay on so the prisoners could get out of their cells and mix with each other a bit. They'd missed out earlier as they had to be locked in while the body was dealt with. It wasn't nice, but I am all right. I believe you just have to get on with things.' Officers and prisoners also had the opportunity of getting psychological support for any trauma they suffered. All deaths in custody were initially treated as suspicious by the police, especially when the late prisoner shared a cell.

Deaths were investigated by the Prisons and Probation Ombudsman who wrote a detailed report that went to the Coroner. This was always followed by an inquest, although there was often a delay of up to eighteen months between the death and the inquest.

Both the report and inquest were testing times for the Prison Governor and staff. Sometimes, as in the case of a Tamil-speaking prisoner in the First Night Centre who committed suicide in January 2008, the prison was found to have done its best and was not blamed or criticised. This was not the case, however, in relation to the suicide of 22-year-old Tony Doherty, who was discovered hanging in his cell in the Segregation Unit in October 2012. The prison was found not to have carried out night patrols in accordance with prison policy, and not to have responded promptly to the cell call bell. CCTV from the night before Doherty's death showed that checks of prisoners on the Segregation Unit had not been completed as required. Despite Doherty ringing his cell bell at 11.55pm, it remained unanswered until he was found at 2.37am, more than 2½ hours later.

Evidence was also heard that for eighteen months prior to the death prison officers could disable the cell's audible alarm, that daily checks of the system were not carried out, nor was a repair requested. One governor who gave evidence for the Prison Service accepted that this was 'totally unacceptable'. The prisoner's mother asked that changes were made so that no other prisoner suffered in the same way. It is no excuse but officers can be under constant pressure for hours on end and when they are severely understaffed the chance of human error inevitably increases.

CHAPTER EIGHT
AT SEA ON DRUGS

The first time I came across drugs in the prison I felt shocked. I was on my rounds in one of the larger wings when I picked up an application from a prisoner who asked to be seen urgently. He had written his name, prison number and details of where to find his cell on the form. It was on the fourth landing so I climbed the three flights of metal stairs, walked down the long corridor until I found the cell number, knocked on the right door, then lifted the observation hatch. This was always a difficult moment as I never knew if the prisoner would be dressed. There were two prisoners in the cell so I called his name, introduced myself, and waited for the right man to come forward.

He was wearing prison-issue tracksuit bottoms but no T shirt. Prisoners are not allowed to leave their cells bare-chested so I suggested he got dressed while I found an officer to unlock the cell. I also needed to find out if it was safe to talk to him outside the cell. Officers have a cell-sized office on each landing as well as a larger one on the ground floor. I was told the prisoner was extremely agitated but not dangerous and I should be OK. It was reassuring that the officer instantly knew who I was talking about.

The prisoner was small and skinny and looked nervously left and right rather like a hunted fugitive as he left the cell. He wanted to talk in private so we walked to the end of the landing where it was relatively quiet. 'I've got to get out of here, Miss,' he began. 'I'm in a real state. Can you help me get to another prison? Otherwise I don't know what I will do. I'm telling you I just can't take it.' He paused then added. 'My gran is up north and can't afford to come and visit me in London. She brought me up and is my only family.' I always tried to adopt the default position when talking to a prisoner to take on board what he said but not at face value. I knew that prisoners can't pick and choose which prison they want to go to, but exceptions can be made on compassionate grounds. He seemed extremely agitated and was trembling with rage.

Transferring from one prison to another was difficult when requested by a prisoner rather than a governor. In addition, some prisons wouldn't take an inmate if they had less than six months of their sentence to run. This prisoner had five months left so it didn't look good. Other prisons wouldn't take inmates who had committed certain crimes. Or they might just be too full. I said I would check with the department responsible for transfers and let him know. Finding out anything in the prison was a challenge, even when a monitor like me could email, ring and search out individuals to talk to. For prisoners it was genuinely frustrating which was why they often turned to us to help. It took a few days to get an answer, which was a firm 'no' as he hadn't met the criteria. I went back to his wing to tell him, worrying how he would react. I couldn't find him in his cell but saw him sauntering along the landing having just collected his lunch.

He smiled when he saw me. 'Hello, Miss,' he began. I told him I was really sorry but I didn't have good news and that it was unlikely that he would be transferred. 'Don't worry,' he replied nonchalantly. 'I decided to go back on heroin instead. Would you like some?' I was speechless and just shook my head. 'Come back whenever you need it,' he beamed. 'And thanks for everything.'

Between seventy and eighty percent of offences are drug-related. Drugs are an endemic problem in prisons and drug addicts made up a significant part of the population in Wormwood Scrubs. Although the prison organised regular drug searches the prisoners showed the sort of initiative in concealing their drugs that I wished they'd applied to staying crime free. Officers told me it was easier to get 'your drug of choice' in a prison than on the street. While a prisoner said: 'You name it and I can get it in here. It is just much more expensive.' One senior manager believed the drug trade in UK prisons was worth about £22million a year. Others have put it at four times that amount. Prisons also had to deal with alcoholism, which is potentially more life-threatening than drug addiction, and with smokers. In 2010 the think tank Policy Exchange did a survey which showed that up to 30,000 prisoners, about 27% of the total prison population, could be taking drugs at any one time, while over 80% of prisoners stated that they could get hold of illicit substances and 20% reported using heroin in jail. At the same time more than half claimed that the easy availability of drugs was preventing them from getting clean and rebuilding their lives.

The battle against drugs at Wormwood Scrubs was two-tiered. One involved new prisoners who were addicts. The other was concerned with the dealing and presence of drugs on the wings themselves. Both were costly and time-consuming. Prisoners who wanted drugs arranged their own deals but often got into debt. I also met prisoners who had been jailed for drug dealing who claimed they carried on dealing in prison, often more profitably. Most drugs could fetch more than seven times their street value. Despite the searches and countless notices around the jail warning of the perils of drug-taking, the prison couldn't eradicate the problem. One senior member of staff told me that as soon as the search officers, with or without dogs, arrived on the ground-floor level of a wing somehow prisoners on the three higher levels got wind of what was happening and got rid of their drugs, he assumed by flushing them down the toilet. I once talked to a senior governor about what needed to be done to stamp drugs out completely. He told me that daily searches had to be undertaken, which there was neither the staff nor budget to do.

- - - - - - - -

One morning I recognised the strong smell of cannabis when I was walking through a wing and sought out the landing officer to tell him. He casually said that there was a current fad amongst prisoners to smoke tea leaves which had a similar smell. I wasn't reassured by this explanation and shortly afterwards told a senior governor the same thing. He rang the wing to ask them to check. I didn't hear anything more. Perhaps I was mistaken. Over time monthly wing reports regularly mentioned 'a strong smell of cannabis' but not what was done about it.

Apart from being illegal anyone high on drugs in a prison was a threat to both other prisoners and staff. Many prisoners bought drugs they couldn't pay for, built up substantial debts, became terrified for their safety and asked to be taken to the Segregation Unit. The prison drug industry also encouraged bullying: dealers pressurised vulnerable prisoners to stash drugs for them in their cell so that if there was a search the supplier didn't get caught.

Illicit drugs reached prisoners in a number of ways. The Visitors' Centre, where prisoners met family and friends, was a regular source despite the presence of officers, sniffer dogs, and compulsory searches for all visitors. In one year one hundred and twenty four visitors were arrested trying to pass drugs. One of the ways was through a loving, lingering kiss. Prisoners and visitors were allowed to kiss on the lips, which was also a good opportunity to pass drugs from mouth to mouth. They could also be wrapped in Clingfilm or in a condom and concealed in a baby's nappy, to be surreptitiously handed over at some point during the visit. Prisoners could hide up to half a kilogram of drugs in their rectum and although they were searched at the end of every visit the Human Rights Act prevents officers touching a man intimately when searching him. However, if officers saw part of a package hanging down, the prisoner was immediately taken to the Segregation Unit.

When officers felt suspicious the prisoner would be ordered to sit on a Body Orifice Security Scanner, better known as a Boss chair that has become significant in the prison's fight against drugs. The £7,000 chair looks like a heavy-duty metal throne but is a highly sensitive metal detector and beeps if a prisoner is hiding drugs, a sim card or mobile in his body. A positive reaction meant a prisoner would be kept in a cell until the object came out naturally. One prisoner insisted that the Boss chair was wrong so officers brought in the prison's specially trained sniffer dogs. They went straight for the prisoner who then gave up his fight. Any prisoners caught with drugs following a visit were prevented, for a specific time, from having open visits and could only speak to their visitors through a screen.

On rare occasions drugs were brought in through the main gate by prison officers or legal staff. Although the vast majority of prison staff were honest one or two were obviously tempted by the financial rewards of drug dealing. A prison officer's starting salary is in the region of £18,000, a year plus £4,000 London allowance, and supplying illicit drugs in prison was perhaps seen as a welcome financial boost.

In March 2009 Patricia Ollivierre, who had worked as a prison officer at Wormwood Scrubs for seven years, was imprisoned for seven years for planning to smuggle drugs into the jail. She was also having an affair with an inmate. She was caught with 17g of heroin and a 51g block of cannabis stashed in her car.

In October 2013 Jason Paul Singh, a 24-year-old officer, was caught trying to smuggle cannabis into the prison. He tried to disguise its distinctive smell by bringing in plenty of vinegar-drenched chips at the same time. He pleaded guilty and was jailed for four years. A few security guards working for Serco the disgraced private-sector company responsible for ferrying prisoners to and from courts have also been arrested on drug issues.

Drugs were also regularly thrown over the prison walls and reeled in by prisoners through their cell windows by a process known as 'fishing.' One memorable package was a large dead pigeon tied up with wire. At the time a prisoner who had been picking up litter was walking through the grounds with a prison officer. He rushed towards what he thought was an injured bird only to be yelled at not to touch it. The pigeon was later found to be stuffed full of heroin. In one month seven parcels containing 11 phones came over the wall along with several chargers and a substantial amount of cannabis.

Other drug parcels, some of which were as big as bricks, were tied up with wire and a metal hook and were usually thrown over at night. The prisoner for whom they were destined was no doubt notified of the impending delivery on his illegal mobile phone. Threads from prison-issue blankets with a wire hook on the end are used to make a 'fishing' line. The prisoner would then smash his cell window to enable him to wind in his catch. Some prisoners were so blasé that subsequently they had the barefaced cheek to complain of draughts.

Copious amounts of wire netting were erected around the more accessible areas of the jail perimeter in the early 2000s to make it more difficult to throw drug and phone parcels over. It worked, but in the winter of 2010/2011 the netting collapsed under the weight of heavy snowfalls, and the number of packages thrown over both day and night sharply increased. There were so many that night patrols were organised to collect them and stop them reaching prisoners. There was also a petition from local residents expressing their annoyance about the number of individuals who came into their gardens to throw packages over the walls. Getting anything replaced or repaired in prison was never quick because of the paperwork and the long delays in getting the authorisation for funds. There was a delay until the end of the financial year in April 2011 before funds could be accessed and the summer was nearly over by the time the netting was finally repaired. The cost was £170,000.

Management wanted to make it more difficult for prisoners to 'fish' through the cell windows. All sorts of preventative measures were suggested, including blocking windows up, changing their shape, and installing bars outside rather than inside. But these plans were rejected by English Heritage because in 2009 the prison cell blocks, chapel and gatehouse were given Grade II listed status. The listing entry states: 'Wormwood Scrubs' was the first "telegraph pole" plan prison in England, probably influenced by hospital plans developed after the Crimean War, and influencing later English as well as French and American prison design. The plan of the prison is thus of national importance, expressed above all by the cell blocks.' A further suggestion on how to alter the windows to stop the 'fishing' was made towards the end of 2013. This was costed at about £1million, which was not viable in the then current financial climate, so it was quietly dropped. The prison, however, regularly spent money on repairing broken windows at a cost per window of £175. Many were then smashed again soon afterwards. In August 2013 the works department was twelve months behind repairing them.

Drugs even arrived by post. Drugs have been found in a cut-out section of a book, in the soft fleshy satin decoration on an old-fashioned birthday card, and even under a postage stamp. Drugs were also brought into the prison by new inmates. The largest hoard of drugs I heard about was a consignment of cocaine, worth on the street about £67,000, that a new prisoner hid internally. It was worth about £500,000 in prison terms, but it was discovered and he was quickly moved onto another prison.

- - - - - - - -

New prisoners delivered to Wormwood Scrubs from police stations or courts were not always honest about their alcohol and drug habits. Many feared further charges and wouldn't trust the medical staff with the information. Prisons did not rely on what a prisoner said and all newcomers were given a urine test to test for drugs in their system. Heavy users, suddenly cut off from their regular substance supply because they were now in prison, could be in a potentially dangerous situation and needed quick medical intervention.

New prisoners with a positive urine test were taken to a specially designated wing fitted out with a calming fish tank and armchairs, which was much smaller, and in theory quieter and less daunting than one of the larger wings. The wing could, however, become very noisy at night when, according to an officer, addicts would 'scream, shout, get very moody and use their cell bells a lot.' Prisoners would subsequently be put on a maintenance programme. About 95% of the addicts were treated with the substitute drug methadone, at a cost of about £2 a time, with the remaining 5% treated with Subutex, which cost about £7 a time. The more expensive Subutex was only given to prisoners who had already been prescribed the drug before they were jailed.

The heavy use of methadone over Subutex caused considerable controversy. Although both drugs took away the severe effects of a heroin habit and eased the symptoms of withdrawal, they were addictive and came with their own withdrawal problems. Methadone, which is more difficult to withdraw from than heroin, is easy to abuse. If too much is taken it can make the user high, which is why it is also sold as a black-market drug. More than 3,000 people die from a methadone overdose each year. Because of the high risk, recovering addicts were given only enough of the drug to last a day and it was always administered under medical supervision. A member of staff from the drug strategy department also attended Reception early each weekday morning to give addicts their dose before they went to court.

A senior governor thought treating prisoners with methadone was ill-advised. 'I really wish we didn't have it in prison,' he admitted. 'I believe it leads to more deaths in custody than anything else. But there is no choice in the matter. It is a national initiative.' Another thoroughly disapproved. 'It's madness for the prison to spend fortunes keeping prisoners drugged up.

Most of them take heroin as well as the substitutes, which makes it doubly a waste of time', while another officer felt that methadone was the better choice for addicts with severe drug problems. As well as being highly addictive, methadone rotted the teeth. One young prisoner showed me his: 'See? I am in my early twenties and I have old man's teeth.'

The detox process was potentially more dangerous for alcoholics. Alcohol withdrawal can be more life threatening than heroin as the body becomes so dependent on alcohol that it goes into withdrawal without it. Seizures appear after about 72 hours and if they are not caught early and treated, alcohol withdrawal can rapidly spiral into a shaking frenzy and death. The standard prison treatment for alcoholics was to put the prisoner on a mood-stabilising drug for about ten days to reduce alcohol craving.

Because of pressure on space in the small wing, addicts usually stayed a maximum of two weeks before being moved to one of the top two floors of a larger wing. By February 2014 there were 130 methadone users in just one wing.

- - - - - - - -

In spring 2008 Pete Doherty, the musician and ex-boyfriend of model Kate Moss, was sent to Wormwood Scrubs for 14 weeks for missing an appointment with his probation officer. The previous October he had been given a suspended sentence for drug and driving offences. Doherty has had a long and public battle with heroin addiction and a picture of him allegedly taking heroin in jail was published by a national tabloid. Days afterwards, officers raided cells in four wings and found significant amounts of heroin, cocaine, Ecstasy and cannabis. They also found substantial amounts of methadone away from the treatment areas. Although a Prison Service spokesman denied it had anything to do with Doherty one source was quoted as saying that Doherty was targeted by the dealers because they could overcharge him. 'Everyone knows Doherty has money. He knows he is being ripped off but all he cares about is a fix.' He added: 'Drug use is rife but key figures who were supplying the whole jail have now been moved and separated, which means the gang culture will hopefully lose its grip.'

I saw Doherty a couple of times while he was in the small treatment wing. Each time he was sitting on one of the armchairs laughing and chatting while surrounded by prisoners who looked as if they couldn't believe their eyes. When Doherty was released after serving 29 days of his sentence he was asked if he had taken drugs while inside. He replied: 'Well, I knew it was going to be a bit rough to start with, with the overcrowding and the medical facilities, although they do their best, they can't really cater for the average junkie.'

One of the services available to prisoners with drug issues was called CARAT: Counselling, Assessment, Referral, Advice and Throughcare. The CARAT workers were meant to work one-to-one with prisoners. Although it sounded promising, there never seemed to be enough of them to deal with all the prisoners who required help, while constant staff changes meant there was little consistency of care. Prisoners sometimes asked monitors to complain that they couldn't see CARAT workers when they needed them. Perhaps I was just unlucky but not once did any member of the CARAT team respond to my phone calls and requests for help or information on behalf of an anxious prisoner.

One prisoner returned to jail because he deliberately broke the terms of his parole, known as a licensed recall, to come back to prison to get help from a CARAT worker for his drug addiction. 'I pleaded guilty to burglary and wanted to be jailed to get some help,' he said. 'My drug of choice is cocaine but when I originally came to prison I went on heroin because there was a lot of strain in my life. I have tried to stop it but it is a struggle. I want to get rid of all my bad drug habits and came to prison to see a CARAT worker and hopefully a psychologist before it is too late.' He was more than disappointed that even seeing a CARAT worker was not going to be easy.

Wormwood Scrubs, in common with all prisons, operated a programme of mandatory drug testing (MDT) for inmates. The prison service order that controlled how this should be done runs to more than 100 pages, so it was an extraordinarily complicated business. The order may get even longer. In June 2013 a bill was put before parliament to enable drug testing to be extended to include abuse of prescription drugs, painkillers, and mood-altering drugs.

Basically, however, the routine was that every few weeks a computer programme randomly selected 6% of the prison population, roughly 84 prisoners, to be tested for drugs. It allowed a certain flexibility over the named prisoners acknowledging that some might have been moved to different prisons or released, so 5%, roughly 64 prisoners, were chosen. Officers could also arrange for specific prisoners to be tested if they suspected they were using drugs. Each prisoner had to supply a urine sample that was divided into two. One half was sent for testing, the other was kept in case the prisoner wanted to challenge the result. The sent sample was then tested for cannabis, cocaine, LSD, heroin, methadone and amphetamines.

Prisoners who couldn't urinate to order were given unlimited amounts of water to drink. If, after five hours they still didn't perform, they were assumed to be guilty and taken to the Segregation Unit. Any randomly selected Muslim prisoner during Ramadan could refuse to drink water as this is not allowed during the day. 'We cannot touch them then' said a member of staff.

Some prisoners were quite cavalier about doing the test, treating it as a form of Russian roulette. 'I work out my drug-taking according to whether I think I'll be tested,' one told me. 'So far I've got it right.' Another who was found to be positive for cocaine was furious. He claimed the prison was treating him like an animal, went on a dirty protest, smashed a sink and toilet in one cell after another and screamed throughout several nights.

Many found the experience daunting. 'I am unhappy about doing a test,' one prisoner confessed. 'I do martial arts so I don't take drugs but I cannot wee in front of anyone no matter how much water I take. I have offered to have a blood test but they won't agree. I feel so stressed out.' After protracted negotiations he was still taken to the Segregation Unit. If a prisoner disputed a positive test, he could get the second sample tested by a body outside the prison at his own expense. Nationality plays a part in those who are most likely to take drugs. In 2012, 52% of those being treated for drugs had a white background – an officer told me Poles took far fewer drugs than English prisoners – 28% came from a black background and 18% from an Asian background. In some cultures, it seems, it is still not the done thing to do drugs

The Ministry of Justice sets a range of performance targets for prisons to reach. The annual target for drug tests for Wormwood Scrubs was that no more than 11.5% of the prisoners should be found to be positive. The actual figure changed each month but when the perimeter netting was down in 2010 and parcels full of drugs were being thrown over the wall, the percentage shot up to 15%. Worryingly the same percentage was reached in the latter months of 2013.

– – – – – – – –

A negative side effect of the mandatory testing was that some prisoners who came to jail with a cannabis habit left addicted to heroin or cocaine. This I was told was partly because cannabis can be detected in the body for up to 30 days, while evidence of heroin and cocaine only lasts one or two days. Some prisoners, anxious that their cannabis habit was not detected tried heroin instead, especially when they were stressed, got hooked, and then often regretted what they had done. One officer commented, 'Many who come in here haven't had a drug problem but get bored and depressed and turn to drugs. I believe the system turns them into addicts.'

Nor did the test give a totally accurate picture. Prisoners on methadone gave a clinically positive result, but once it was noted they had been given the drug by the healthcare team, the result was automatically cancelled. Hardy prisoners knew this and saw it as an opportunity to take heroin along with their methadone.

Whatever the statistics and targets, addicts rarely kick their habit in jail and nowhere near enough is done to address their problem. What therapy there is, is spread far too thin and the treatment is an exercise in marking time. In the past, addicts were helped to give up drugs entirely, but that is now rarely the case. In 2006, nearly 200 prisoners and former inmates from jails round the country who had been using heroin and other opiates claimed that being forced to go 'cold turkey' amounted to an assault and breached their human rights. The Home Office agreed to settle out of court, reportedly to minimise the cost to the taxpayer, and each prisoner received about £11,000.

The other reason why prisons keep addicts on a heroin substitute is, ironically to help save their lives. When addicts leave prison many go back to their former habit and take drugs at roughly the same level they did before they were jailed. If they have been given lower doses of a substitute to reduce their dependency, their body is often unable to cope with the higher amount and several have died over the years as a result of overdosing.

A recent study by King's College London found that the risk of a drugs-related death is 7.5 times higher in the first fortnight after a prisoner is released than at any other time. It also revealed that one in 200 released prisoners with a history of heroin injection died from a drugs-related cause within four weeks of leaving prison. As a result, the amount of methadone a prisoner was given just before his release, was approximately the same level as his original habit. My personal view is that it is a form of legal collusion with the addicts and shocking that both the Coalition and Prison Service perpetuate drug use in this way.

There were differing views amongst the staff. One officer said: 'If we have someone in custody for over a year I don't think it is right to put them on maintenance. We can do that to start with but they should subsequently be detoxed. I don't agree that before they go out they should then be put up to the level they were on before they came to prison even if it is a human rights issue. Long-term prisoners kept on maintenance are often increasingly difficult to manage and we need a better policy.'

Another agreed with the maintenance programme: 'Crash withdrawal is inhuman and it is degrading forcing someone to have unpleasant and degrading symptoms,' he said.

A prisoner complained to me that his methadone dose had been increased. He had self-harmed the previous day and alleged the prison doctor had increased his methadone to deal with his distress. 'I don't want to be on that,' he said. 'I don't want it used as a painkiller. I want to get clean. I have two months left of my sentence and wanted to be clean before I go out. I don't want to be an addict any more. I would rather go cold turkey but they won't let me.'

Hardened smokers were another problem. About 80% of prisoners smoked, but they were only allowed to light up in their cell or in the yard outside their wing. A proportion complained about the attention drug addicts received compared to smokers and demanded more help with their addiction. I went to see one prisoner who had written that he had a health issue to discuss. He was reading a book about the Great Train Robbery of 1963 when I arrived at his cell. He felt angry and badly treated. 'If you are a junkie they put you on a special programme,' he began. 'I want to give up smoking, but where are my smoking patches? I am entitled to them and if I don't get them soon I will contact my solicitor. They are just not helping me give up.' I explained that he could get patches from the healthcare team and attend a Narcotics Anonymous group once a week, but there wasn't much personal counselling available. He insisted it was the prison's responsibility to get him off cigarettes. It was a typical prisoner's stance: not accepting responsibility for his own actions, along with throwing out a threat if his issue wasn't sorted out.

Prisoners can be very resourceful. I was told some of them used their nicotine patches purely to make cigarettes. This apparently involved boiling them in water to extract the nicotine, then soaking teabags, fruit peel and even fluff from a tumble drier in the water. This was left to dry, then shredded to make a type of cigarette.

Things may get worse for the smoker. The Prison Service has become concerned that it may face compensation claims from prisoners alleging they have been affected by passive smoking. As a result, a pilot scheme of a total smoking ban was planned to start in 2014 with a full ban likely to come into force by 2015. A total ban might be difficult for prison officers as well as inmates: many of them volunteered to supervise prisoners taking exercise outside so they could have a quick smoke.

CHAPTER NINE
UNHEALTHY OBSESSIONS

I t was astonishing to discover how many prisoners were obsessed with their health and how uninhibited they could be about divulging intimate, stomach-churning details of ailments both big and small to me, a stranger. Urine issues was a particularly popular topic. With so little to do, prisoners' problems assumed enormous significance and understandably they often made a huge fuss about something quite minor. They were childishly grateful for any reassurance, but could also get very angry when a member of the medical team didn't do exactly what they wanted.

'There's a build-up of skin between one of my toes,' one prisoners told me dramatically. 'I think it might be a soft corn. It's really bad and they won't let me see the doctor. Please help me.' I suggested he asked to be put on the list to see the podiatrist. Another was beset with haemorrhoids and desperate to see the doctor. I did my best to get him further up the waiting list but was told firmly: 'He may very well be in pain, but it is not an emergency.'

Certain prisoners saw some sort of skullduggery in every aspect of prison life. 'I need stronger painkillers' said one, 'I am going crazy with pain. Mark my words there's a lot more to the low-dose prescription than you might think.'

Overall their attitude to their health was much the same as to other areas of their lives. It was the responsibility of someone else – doctor/optician/dentist/hospital – to sort out. Although a minority of prisoners liked keeping fit and eating healthily, the majority didn't look after themselves or have much idea of basic healthcare. They did, however, know all about drugs. They would reel off various different names of medication they claimed they had been prescribed before they were jailed and demanded the same from prison doctors. I had many applications from prisoners protesting that the doctors prescribed less strong or different medication to what they alleged they were used to. Their complaints regularly included that the doctor 'didn't know what he was talking about.'

One wrote: 'The doctors are discriminating against me by refusing me medication. I feel victimised and my duty of care is being infringed.' Another was concerned that although his medication was supposed to be administered every six hours he claimed he was offered two doses within an hour of each other. He said he mentioned this 'politely' to the nurse who allegedly replied: 'There is nothing I can do.' I went to see the nurse on his behalf and discovered what the prisoner said was true. I was told it was due to staff shortages. This was far from best medical practice.

A prisoner willingly shared the background to his chronic ill- health. He told me: 'I am not mentally ill. I'm a chronic self-harmer with learning difficulties who was emotionally and physically abused as a child. I currently need (a particular medication) to stop me hallucinating.'

'When prisoners don't get their own way with medication they can be very rude,' a member of the health team told me. 'I tell them it is never acceptable to raise their voice when they are being treated. The trouble is their expectations of how they should be treated are not always realistic. They demand everything they want free from the NHS.'

Not all of them could be trusted to self-medicate. One prisoner complained furiously that he was being denied medication for his asthma. On paper and in person his grievance sounded justified, but, as often happened, he hadn't told the whole story. I was informed by a healthcare worker that he had 'abused' the medication and finished it in one go when it was supposed to last for four months. She added, 'He wasn't even having an asthmatic attack.' I was told he would continue to receive medication when necessary but was no longer trusted to take it himself.

Some prisoners tried to bully the doctors, especially if they were locums, to provide the drugs they wanted, which could then be traded within the jail. The Chief Inspector of Prisons Nick Hardwick told the House of Commons Justice Committee in February 2014: 'Healthcare staff bring them (drugs) in and hand them out to a queue of prisoners and then they become a tradeable commodity or a bulliable commodity.'

Prisoners' irritation over medication covered both major and minor ailments, ranging from heart care and cancer to headaches and being unable to sleep. Alleged insomnia was always a tricky one as countless numbers of prisoners, including those in their twenties, would spend large parts of the day asleep in their cells. It was no surprise that they couldn't sleep at night.

The high turnover of prisoners at Wormwood Scrubs made it difficult to deal with their health issues, especially when they had chronic diseases.

Almost ten percent of prisoners had asthma, which was about two per cent higher than residents in the vicinity of the prison. The higher statistic applied to smokers and those who came from a socially deprived group, which most prisoners belonged to. Smoking and asthma also left prisoners more at risk of other pulmonary illnesses. Hepatitis B, hepatitis C and HIV were prevalent and tuberculosis was a growing public health threat. All monitors were encouraged to have inoculations against TB and hepatitis, 'not least,' we were told, 'because you come into close proximity with prisoners and they could spit at you.' An ever-growing serious issue was the increasing number of mentally ill prisoners, both those who were severely ill and those who had less acute or treatable mental health problems but who still needed support.

— — — — — — —

Prior to April 2003, prisons were responsible for their own primary healthcare services. They employed the staff and could investigate problems and, if necessary, take action to improve or change personnel or practices. However, the Prison Service decided it was operating with 'significant weaknesses' and following countless initiatives and policy documents dating back to 1996, in 2003 the NHS finally took over responsibility for prison healthcare. A joint statement by the NHS and Prison Service stated at the time that their principle was: 'To give prisoners access to the same quality and range of health care services as the general public.'

In the following ten years the Ministry of Justice was established, Primary Care Trusts were abolished and any number of reviews and mission statements produced. Since April 2013 the healthcare services in all prisons in England have been run by a partnership between the National Offender Management Services (NOMS), which reports to the Ministry of Justice, NHS England and Public Health England. To add to the complexity, healthcare in Wormwood Scrubs itself was taken over by the Central London Community Healthcare NHS Trust (CLCH) in January 2011.

It didn't change the level of complaints. Most years the monitoring board received more complaints about healthcare issues than about anything else in the prison. Unlike the population at large who struggle with NHS waiting lists and staff shortages, many prisoners had no patience to wait and often complained that their human rights were being abused if they couldn't see the medic they needed straight away. An officer was correct when he told me: 'The big problem with healthcare is that the people who shout the loudest are the ones who get seen first.' It was another example of how prison is the survival of the fittest.

Prisoners also regularly submitted complaints about the amount of attention they received and the attitude of staff. One prisoner who claimed to have bowel cancer stated categorically that the prison medical team was not giving him any help. I checked with a health worker, who looked through his notes and told me the dates he had been seen by a member of the health team: I felt reassured that he was being regularly looked after. To protect his privacy, the health worker neither confirmed nor denied the prisoner's diagnosis. Another agitated prisoner who alleged he had mouth cancer that had spread to his brain complained he wasn't getting strong enough analgesics to help with the pain in his face. The doctor told me he was prescribing what he felt was the correct dosage.

Another complained about the attitude of a nurse: 'She has an aggressive manner and is discriminating against me, refusing me medication and treating me like a drug addict, which I am not.' He went on to add a well-used line about his 'rights'. 'I feel victimised and that my duty of care is being infringed.' He demanded her removal.

Although there was a well-established process for prisoners to follow if they wanted to complain about something that happened in the jail, it was genuinely harder to get answers to complaints about healthcare as it was run by the NHS rather than the prison. Complaints about clinical and non-clinical matters had to be processed through NHS England, which was both complex and lengthy. Equally significantly concerns about a GP, specialist or nurse could only be processed by the NHS rather than the prison. One doctor for example had a problem writing out prescriptions correctly. On occasion the care was so poor that staff would complain in their monthly wing reports. These included concerns about 'inconsistent' care for a prisoner with stomach cancer and one who had a colostomy.

- - - - - - - -

Healthcare in Wormwood Scrubs operated at various levels. Most wings had a small medical facility where prisoners were seen by a doctor or nurse and could collect medication. There was a large outpatient unit some distance from the wings where prisoners from all the wings were taken for appointments with various specialists ranging from urologists to opticians. There was also a small residential healthcare unit for prisoners with serious mental illness or complex health needs, which fairly or not reminded me of a Victorian mental asylum. Prisoners who needed scans, specialist tests, operations or emergency care were usually taken to Hammersmith Hospital, which was close by.

Common complaints from prisoners about the wing health units were that they couldn't always see the doctor or nurse when they wanted to, that the nurses were 'patronising' and the doctors 'intimidating', 'uncaring' or treated the prisoner 'like shit.' One prisoner who alleged he had seriously damaged the main arteries on his arms by self-harming called the doctor 'utterly useless' because he prescribed a different pain killer to the one he claimed his local GP had given him. 'I shall complain to my solicitor' he threatened.

The day care unit was criticised for its waiting lists. On average these could be five weeks for podiatry, five weeks for an optician, four weeks for an urologist, and eight–ten weeks for the dentist. Prisoners were notoriously bad at looking after their teeth. It was also difficult to find NHS dentists to work in the prison and those that could often chose to work part-time.

I met several youthful prisoners who, when they talked, revealed a mouthful of decayed brown teeth more fitting to a Dickensian villain than a young man in the 21st century. One angrily told me he had come into prison to get his teeth fixed and only had four weeks to get them sorted, so would I get him to the top of the list.

Another complained that he was in constant pain with a wisdom tooth. He said: 'I have been waiting weeks to see the dentist but no one here does anything to help you.' A third said he had had toothache for eight weeks and found it difficult to eat and sleep. A fourth claimed he had a 'terribly painful' abscess on a tooth. I wasn't sure who made the diagnosis of an abscess but passed on all problems to the relevant department because there was some flexibility for a genuine emergency.

Prisoners were as paranoid about healthcare as they were about other aspects of prison life and often grumbled they were kept on a waiting list deliberately to prolong their pain. I tried to reassure them that this was most unlikely and explained that it was difficult to find enough doctors to meet the demand. This simple explanation often re-assured them and was a helpful reminder that monitors had a role in giving prisoners straightforward information that prison officers had no time to do.

It was a revelation, therefore, to discover after all the fuss how many prisoners didn't in the end bother to turn up for their appointments. In one month alone there were 150 no-shows at the prison's outpatients department including for the dentist. This inevitably increased waiting lists as the way the prison functioned made it impossible to replace a patient at the last minute. Prisoners can't wander around a prison on their own for obvious security reasons and are accompanied by officers to and from the healthcare unit in a group from individual wings.

When a prisoner complained they hadn't been seen by a doctor and their medical issue was getting worse I always checked on the appointments list. On almost every occasion over many years I discovered that he had not shown up for his appointments. When I mentioned this not one of them seemed to grasp the connection between not turning up, feeling worse and an increased waiting list. Sometimes they simply forgot. In the outside world huge numbers of motivated, responsible adults forget about medical appointments, but when people are confined in one place like a prison it shouldn't have been difficult to get them to turn up or at least notify the relevant specialist in good time so that someone else could take their place.

Administrative failures in the system didn't help. Each day wing officers were given separate lists of what prisoners were booked to do, for example go on a visit, go to the gym, attend a workshop, or see their lawyer. These lists were neither co-ordinated nor checked for double bookings and prisoners were allowed to decide at the last minute to go, for example, to the gym rather than the doctor.

The monitoring board highlighted the problem of medical no-shows in 2010. The prison management agreed it was a serious issue and said things would change but changes in prisons never happen quickly. Just under four years later a 'mission statement' was completed. Extracts read: 'The partnership group has taken this (medical no shows) up. There is discussion about how to centrally manage movements... There is no capacity at present for prisoners to effect their appointments and no cancellation pathways... The wing healthcare representative role will involve delivering slips and reminding prisoners....'

More time was wasted with a survey. Prisoners were asked to fill out a form 'stating reason for missing appointments which could then be audited for service improvement.' This was, apparently, only a 'limited success due to illiteracy issues with prisoners.'

By March 2014 we were still waiting. It seems extraordinary in a computer age when individual lists can be cut and pasted on to a master list in less than a minute, then emailed round to members of staff who needed to see it, that it could take so long to sort out something so straightforward. Even in a prison.

Recruiting medical staff including nurses was difficult, not least because prison is not an appealing environment. All staff needed security clearance. They also risked being threatened or attacked by an inmate. Locum doctors and psychiatrists were regularly used. One member of the medical team decided quite quickly it wasn't the right job for him. 'There are a lot of prisoners here with personality disorders of various sorts and there is not very good provision for them in prison. Others are just badly behaved and anti-social. I cannot accept this anti-social behaviour, nor the way these guys have a technique of really alienating you and making you feel you are no good at your job. There needs to be a multidiscipline team and a management plan so that as well as dealing with any physical problems there are also therapeutic activities that are put in place for prisoners to have one-to-one attention with a psychiatrist, nurse or prison officer.'

In practice this was difficult as staff vacancy rates, particularly for nurses, could soar to fifty per cent. Chronic staff shortages not only affected waiting lists but also made it more difficult for staff to deal with a demanding workload. On occasion prisoners' lives were put at risk. The prison was sharply criticised following a death in the healthcare unit in 2009.

Agency nurses were regularly used to cover, which was very expensive. In one month alone £160,000 was spent on temporary nurses. Towards the end of 2010, monitors received an increased number of applications from prisoners who complained that nurses were uncaring, brutal and not interested in them. It was important to investigate these complaints, rather than assume they were just bad feeling. Senior administrative staff were concerned about some nurses attitude and agreed it was never acceptable for a member of the medical team to raise their voice when dealing with a prisoner, whatever the provocation. Efforts were subsequently made to cut down on agency nurses and instead temporary nurses were hired from a central pool organised by the Central London Community Healthcare NHS Trust. From January 2011 they provided services to the prison. As a result prisoner care, both pastoral and physical improved.

-- -- -- -- -- -- -- --

Prisoners who were mentally ill or had multifaceted health needs were treated in a small 17-bed residential wing within the healthcare unit that had windowless internal single cells, a dormitory and a special care unit. It was managed by a mix of prison officers and nursing staff and there were regular visits from psychiatrists and doctors. Before going round the wing I had to sign in at the main office. It is an understatement to say some of the prisoners were difficult. A nurse or officer in the main office would tell me who I should physically steer well clear of. For example, I could be told to avoid walking close to one cell as the prisoner was likely to throw urine and faeces at anyone who passed by. I should avoid another as he was going through a violent patch and might try to grab me by the neck.

The wing itself was a dark, gloomy place. I found it the most depressing area of the prison and often felt concerned that I might contract some unpleasant disease. I felt particularly uneasy that severely mentally and physically unwell prisoners were mixed together in one unit. It was something that does not happen elsewhere in the NHS. The independent monitors pointed out several times in our annual report to the Justice Secretary that we did not believe this helped the recovery of prisoners in either group.

Prisoners were sent to the unit on a daily basis. In one representative month admissions included seven prisoners who had mental health issues, two who were serious self-harmers, two who were physically unwell and one who was extremely vulnerable. Walking round the unit was profoundly disheartening. A mentally ill prisoner could be pounding round his almost empty cell, while another was in a foetal position in a corner. A third could be lying motionless on a fixed bed or staring through the open flap of the cell with wild, unseeing eyes. There was nothing for them to read, listen to or watch in their cells. Televisions and radios were potentially dangerous objects they could smash and use to harm others or themselves; there were no TV in the cells but there were a couple in the communal area of the wing. The unpredictability and bouts of sudden aggression that characterised many of the severely mentally ill made them extremely difficult to cope with and they couldn't be trusted out of their cells.

– – – – – – – –

The number of registered mental health prisoners in Wormwood Scrubs regularly reached nearly 700 of whom only one or two were transferred out of the prison per month. This is despite national guidelines which set the target that severely mentally unwell prisoners should be transferred within fourteen days to 'an appropriate community setting'. The reality is that this can't be done as mental health units are bursting at the seams and when there is space they specifically choose what type of mental illness they will take. Getting agreement to move these prisoners was often a slow process and although a dribble of inmates were moved over time to a secure environment, in January and February 2013 for example, not one single prisoner left the prison for an NHS facility.

The truth is that if mentally unwell prisoners were moved to a proper facility the prison would be less than half full. Instead the severely mentally ill regularly stayed in the healthcare unit for months at a time and the prison had the onerous task of keeping them safe from others and themselves. About 30% of the inmates with psychiatric issues also suffered from depression.

Because the prison did not have a psychiatric unit with proper facilities and staff, the prison could, at best, offer a holding operation. One of the medical team explained: 'Staff tell me about difficult prisoners all the time. There are so many very disturbed people here and no resources to deal with them. They should be having intense treatment from psychiatrists and psychologists. Instead they are left on their own with their troubled thoughts. They are then released at the end of their sentence totally unable to cope on the outside, commit a crime and are brought back again.

'This unit is called a hospital but it isn't. It is a place where we observe, monitor and hold men with serious psychiatric conditions. Ninety percent of the people here are awaiting transfer to secure accommodation and they are too bad or too unwell to be on the wings. We sometimes try with a prisoner but many are very unpredictable and if they suddenly become very aggressive they have to be brought back.

'Every decision is a difficult one. One prisoner continually veers from being very needy to extremely demanding and when he is let out of his cell often becomes threatening and intimidating. He has recently broken several toilets. Another, who is desperately unwell, ripped up the floor. He has also threatened to smash my face and is very difficult with non-white members of staff.'

Very occasionally, one of these prisoners would leave an application for the monitors in the green metal box. Sadly, nearly all those I picked up were incomprehensible. I would talk to the prisoner to try to understand the problem.

The staff had particular problems dealing with prisoners who behaved as if they were mad, but were declared sane by psychiatrists. In other words, the professionals felt he was acting for his own purposes. Regular staff noticed that the behaviour of one of these prisoners deteriorated if he was about to be deported or had a court hearing. At other times he seemed almost normal, he would engage with staff then suddenly attack an officer or himself.

It was hard to cope with men like him. Not least because if they had a mental illness they could go on a waiting list for a place in a suitable hospital unit. As it was, the most staff could hope for was that at some point another prison would agree to swap them for someone they wanted to get rid of.

When any these men became particularly disruptive or violent they would be taken down, usually by four officers wearing protective gear, to the Segregation Unit. Segregation officers do not however have specific training to deal with severely mentally ill prisoners but had to cope as best they could. Over subsequent weeks these prisoners could go back and forth between the two units as demand on the space allowed. It was no way to treat a human being, and particularly someone seriously unwell.

Because there were so many of them, slightly less disturbed mentally ill prisoners were placed on one or more wings. Most were thought unfit to share a cell so were left on their own in a single cell. One officer commented: 'I feel for the mentally ill prisoner in a general wing. I am passionate about my job, I care how they are treated and know prison isn't the right place for them. It is not their fault that there isn't space in the healthcare unit and most commit offences because of the mental state they are in.'

The small healthcare unit included special cells where prisoners who were at risk of suicide could be constantly monitored. These included prisoners who had, for example, been caught making a ligature, hoarding medication, or had written a suicide note, and/or had already attempted suicide. Checks were always made to ensure there was nothing in these cells that could be used to self-harm or as an aid to suicide. Temporary nursing assistants were employed to sit in an armchair just outside these open cells to watch the prisoner constantly and make regular notes of their observations. National prison policy was that this intense observation should only be used for the shortest time possible, as the prisoner had no privacy. The relevant prison service order stated: 'the process of being constantly supervised by a member of staff can be de-humanising, which may increase risk.' Choosing when to stop these observations was not easy. Suicidal prisoners who were also violent were kept in special cells with a barred metal gate that allowed constant supervision and prevented them from leaving their cell.

Shortages of staff affected cell watchers as they did other aspects of healthcare; sometimes with tragic results. In April 2009 a Muslim prisoner from Azerbaijan hanged himself in a gated cell after only seven days in the prison, six of which were spent in the healthcare unit. He had declared he would die in prison when he arrived at Reception so he was assessed as being 'at risk' and put on a special watch. He was given an anti-tear blue gown to wear and two anti-tear blankets designed so that they couldn't be used as a ligature. On the afternoon and evening of the day of his death, the unit was very short-staffed and the prisoner was not supervised all the time as another suicidal prisoner was brought into the unit.

He was last observed at 6pm but was discovered hanging from pipes in the cell less than an hour later. He had managed to tear a strip from the 'non-tear' blanket and attached it to pipes in the ceiling. Pipes in these specialist cells were supposed to be boxed in to prevent prisoners tying a ligature round them, but in this case the plastic box wasn't flush to the ceiling. As soon as he was discovered a defibrillator machine was used. This sends electrical impulses to the heart and advises whether there is any rhythm that might be stimulated. Sadly soon afterwards he was pronounced dead. The subsequent report by the Prisons and Probation Ombudsman criticised the prison's safer custody procedures, the then senior Governor and the head of healthcare. It was one of three deaths in custody at Wormwood Scrubs that year.

Prisoners who needed hospital treatment were handcuffed and accompanied by at least two prison escorts. Leaving the prison for any reason always offered a prisoner a chance to escape and when in 2007 Joe Farnan, then 27, who was serving life for firearm offences, was taken down the road from Wormwood Scrubs to Hammersmith Hospital he was accompanied by three prison escorts and two ambulance workers. When the ambulance pulled into A & E, however, three men wearing balaclavas, one of whom was carrying a firearm, forced open the doors and ordered the guards to unlock the prisoner's handcuffs. He was then rushed into a waiting car, which sped off. The prison guards were subsequently treated for shock. A few days later Farnan was arrested in London Docklands. It was believed he faked fits in order to dupe nurses and doctors into calling for an ambulance.

One prisoner whom I was asked to see took great exception to the security aspect of going to hospital. 'A prison guard sat handcuffed to me while I went in for my consultation with the doctor,' he told me. 'It was appalling. I didn't want him to overhear confidential information that was intended just for the doctor.' I explained there was nothing I could do about fundamental security issues so he decided not to follow up with any more out-patient appointments until after his release. Providing escorts, and the number varied per month between 40 and 70, was heavy on staff and expensive. There had to be two guards at a time, which meant six were needed for a prisoner for one overnight stay in hospital.

-- -- -- -- -- -- -- --

In 2011 about £55,000 was donated, largely by the King's Fund charity, to create a therapy room in an unused area of the healthcare unit. The prison donated £10,000 for furniture. A couple of sofas, a large flat-screen communal television and some tables and chairs, fixed for safety reasons to the floor, arrived. It was thought it would encourage the less dangerous or ill prisoners to socialise during lunch or the evening meal. I never saw them used when I was in the unit and very few prisoners watched television.

The therapy room, however, became invaluable. A series of folding doors enabled the room to be used for one-to-one therapy, group therapy, relaxing techniques such as yoga, art classes, and anger management and stress management training. These classes often formed part of what was called Wellbeing Day that looked at healthy lifestyles. A significant percentage of the prisoners were too dangerous or mentally ill to take advantage of what was on offer but it was something positive to do for the rest. The renovation was an improvement but didn't counteract the overall depressing environment of the unit or help the most vulnerable.

At the end of 2011 work began to convert one of the two dormitories in the healthcare unit to accommodate two or three acute primary care beds. The money, amounting to six figures, came out of the NHS budget. It was seen as a potential money saver as well as a way to reduce pressure on staff as fewer prisoners would need hospital treatment. Or at the very least be looked after for longer within the prison both before and after going to hospital. It was hoped it could also provide a more therapeutic environment for prisoners who were dying, monitor prisoners suffering from unstable acute conditions like asthma and diabetes and care for disabled prisoners. It was barely used and following the cuts of October 2013, was also deemed to be too expensive to run. What a waste of money.

CHAPTER TEN
FOOD FOR ALL

An experienced prison officer told me that the two most important things for a prisoner were food and maintaining links with his family. 'If you don't muck about with that, prisoners will tolerate almost anything,' he said. 'Family contact should never be under-estimated. It is often, in the end, the key motivation for someone to go straight.' At Wormwood Scrubs a prisoner's family could contact him by mail and email and come in person for a pre-arranged visit. Each option required effort and a certain amount of tenacity. Visits were the most complicated. It is not possible to turn up to see a prisoner on the spur of the moment.

Remand prisoners were allowed more visits than convicted prisoners. The latter were allocated between two and four visits a month, depending on their crime and how well they conformed to prison routine. Arranging a visit required both perseverance and patience. A convicted prisoner needed to fill in a visiting order with the details of his visitor. This was then checked and approved by Security before being posted to the applicant. Prisoners complained regularly that their orders never arrived at their destination, sometimes when they hadn't actually filled anything in. Blaming the post room often turned out to be an easy way of avoiding seeing someone. I spent some time trying to trace these orders only for the inmate to finally confess he'd used the stamp money for tobacco instead. Prisoners could choose who they wanted to see, but were not necessarily allowed to see everyone they wanted to.

One asylum-seeker was very concerned that the ten visiting orders he alleged he had completed over several weeks had all been refused. 'They won't allow me to see my three-year-old daughter,' he said angrily. 'She means so much to me.' I checked. It turned out that social services wouldn't let him to see her because he was guilty of sex crimes. He was not, however, barred from having adult visitors. This made him angry. 'I am not in prison for sex crimes this time,' he insisted.

Another prisoner resented the fact that he had been stopped from having visits because he had been caught with a mobile phone. 'I know all about that,' he said, 'but I need the support of my current partner and I can't go on without seeing my mother, who has a heart condition.' Of course if these men hadn't committed a crime, these situations could have been avoided.

Several inmates were furious when they were only allowed to have closed visits. This meant speaking to their visitor behind a screen and no physical contact. One said: 'I have a 10-week-old baby who I want to bond with plus three other children and I don't want to be put in a box. I have put in two complaints so far.' He refused to acknowledge that the reason for the closed visits was that drugs had recently been passed on to him by mouth from one of his visitors.

Once a visiting order arrived it was then up to the visitor to contact the prison to fix a time and date. This was never easy, as visiting slots on any given day were quickly filled. It helped that foreign national prisoners rarely had family in London otherwise booking a visit would have been even more difficult. The slots for legal visits also filled up extremely fast.

There was never a time when there were no complaints about the prison phone system, which was usually a shambles. For several months in 2007 there was a backlog of 120 legal visits, as well as a severe delay for social visits while one booking clerk 'took a career break.' The following year an anxious mum posted a plea on the Mumsnet website asking if anyone had advice on how to get through to the switchboard at the Scrubs visiting centre as all three phone lines had been constantly engaged for three days.

Visitors also complained of being cut off and/or not being able to leave a message when they got through. Over one Christmas period the visiting line was closed from noon on 24 December until 2 January. Unhelpfully the message on the answerphone merely said the line was closed and not when it would reopen. When a would-be visitor managed to get through, a staff member had to obtain a vast amount of detailed information, so calls were never quick. They could also be expensive if made from a mobile rather than a landline. Delays in processing the visits became so bad that the Governor moved several admin members of staff from different parts of the prison into the department to catch up and man the lines. Those returning from sick leave, or confined to light duties also found themselves dealing with visits. It was then discovered that one of the reasons for the complaints about not getting through was because staff didn't know how to handle the answerphone, so didn't access the messages. Some speedy training was organised. It's indicative to me how the prison is so bogged down with procedures and prison service orders that initiative is crushed. In 2011 booking by email was introduced which slightly eased the situation. Unfortunately that system kept crashing too.

-- -- -- -- -- -- -- --

In June 2011, Spurgeons, a children's charity, sponsored a new purpose-built, family-friendly visiting centre in an outbuilding of the prison. This was officially opened by Crispin Blunt MP, then Minister for Prisons. It was a very welcome facility even though only 42 visitors could be accommodated at any one time, which was not much for such a large prison. Nonetheless it was a huge improvement on the visitors centre it replaced, which had had a filthy, worn carpet and chairs with torn upholstery that revealed grubby foam underneath. The new centre was clean, modern, colourful with tables and chairs, a children's mini-playground and a canteen.

All visitors were searched on arrival at the jail to make sure they didn't have illicit items. They were, however, allowed to take in up to £20 for refreshments. Administrative errors, when details of the visit weren't passed on to the prisoner or relevant wing, were the cause of many visits not taking place. An inmate's family, who could have travelled far, could wait for a prisoner, who didn't know a visit had been fixed. It was not good for family relations. Because of the nature of a prison and security issues it is not possible to ring a wing, find out what was going on and get the prisoner brought to the centre. Nor did all visits between a prisoner and his girlfriend, partner or wife go well. There were sometimes arguments that turned violent and some prisoners were arrested for assault.

It could also be difficult for prisoners to make phone calls. They couldn't ring anyone in case the individual was a victim or witness of their crime and could be intimidated or bullied. The chance to ring whoever they wanted to was a key reason why prisoners paid well over the odds for a mobile. The public phones on each wing could only be operated with a unique pin number, which was given to every prisoner shortly after he arrived at the jail. The procedure was he then put money into his personal account and gave staff a list of any personal numbers he wished to call, and those for his lawyer. It was rarely as straightforward as it sounds. All prisoners had to hand in their mobiles when they arrived. These were then stored with the rest of their personal property in a vast property department at the prison. Nowadays most people make calls by clicking on an individual's name rather than remembering a number. The property area was a long walk from the cells and staff weren't readily available to go backwards and forwards with countless prisoners who wanted to retrieve some phone numbers.

In addition, every phone number on a prisoner's list had to be checked by a clerk to make sure that the individual at the other end wanted to have contact with the prisoner. Landlines cost less for prisoners to call than mobiles but had the disadvantage that the person was less likely to be in during the day, especially if they were at work when the number was checked. Meanwhile the clerks who checked the lines only worked a 9am-5pm day. If they didn't get a response to their check call after a day or two, the reaction of some was to put the list at the bottom of the pile of work in hand to be dealt with at another time.

It could take anything from a few days to several weeks before a prisoner could make a call. There was even one period when prisoners had to wait months for their phone numbers to be cleared due to acute shortage of staff and a peak of illness. One employee admitted he had a two feet high pile of forms waiting for attention. It was frustrating for prisoners and something I could occasionally speed up. Prisoners prone to paranoia wrongly felt the delay was deliberately against them. 'This prison has colluded and conspired to make sure that I am not able to make any phone calls to my lawyer,' one claimed. 'I believe it has been surreptitiously done to make sure I receive no legal representation.'

Another demanded a video link between two prisons so he could speak to his girlfriend as his attempts to call her had failed. Video links were mainly used to enable a prisoner to make a court appearance without leaving the prison rather than for personal use.

'Me coming to prison made her homeless,' he told me. 'She is now in prison herself, and was stopped from hanging herself by the skin of her teeth. Now they've told me they are shipping me out to another prison but I swear on my father's grave and my children's life that I didn't try to escape. The accusation is making me crack up and has triggered such a nervous reaction in my head that I have also felt like harming myself and giving up on life, which is really not like me.' I tended to take such intense stories of woe, initially at least, with several pinches of salt and tried to find out whether a prisoner was relating the most dramatic story he could think of to manipulate a situation or whether a combination of disasters had reduced him to despair. I told him I didn't know if video links between prisoners were allowed but that I would check with the senior officer on his wing.

Prisoners could also only make calls at specific times during the day. It was extremely difficult to call in the evening once they were locked up for the night. Nor was there much privacy. With little to occupy their mind, a phone home could become the focus of a prisoner's day and if he couldn't make the call he could easily over react, especially if he was feeling vulnerable. Several prisoners claimed they had self-harmed because they couldn't speak to a member of their family. One prisoner with bandaged arms from cutting himself explained. 'I slashed myself because it's become impossible to talk to my aunt who is my closest family member because she doesn't get home from work until the evening. I really need to speak to her.'

Some prisoners kept in touch by letter. About five sacks of mail arrived at the prison six mornings a week and both incoming and outgoing mail was checked for its contents by the censors. It was also checked for drugs, cash and inflammatory language that could encourage a riot. All mail was stamped with the date it arrived and there was always a steady number of complaints from prisoners who said that they had waited sometimes as long as six days for their letter to come from the post room to the wing. It was another sign of inefficiency and staff shortages. Prisoners also complained that letters they wrote never arrived at their destination. Security in the post room was so tight that even IMB members, who had access to almost every nook and cranny in the prison, were not allowed inside, unless it was essential and arranged in advance.

More recently prisoners could be contacted by email via the emailaprisoner service. The email would be printed, its contents checked by officers and delivered once a day to the prisoner. The prisoner couldn't respond by email for security reasons. One prisoner's girlfriend complained that her emails didn't reach her lover quickly enough. It turned out she was bombarding him with emails all day and expected each one to be delivered at the time it was sent.

- - - - - - - -

The other most important thing for a prisoner was food. This was recognised by an astonishing 75-page prison service order. It stated: 'Providing meals and food for prisoners is a key issue in maintaining order and control and statistics show that out of the Prison Service's total expenditure of £94million in 2004-2005, £43 million was spent on food.' The order went into extraordinary detail about every aspect of prison food, including such helpful comments as 'The term sandwich refers to any filled bread or like product...' It was another example of the bureaucracy that characterises the public sector.

An inmate might well have not cared much about what he ate on the outside but once in prison meal times and food almost invariably became a major issue, not least because they helped to break up the monotony of life in jail. It was an incredible operation to prepare three meals a day for more than 1,200 prisoners on a budget of £1.87 per prisoner per day. There also had to be five choices of main course, which was surely unnecessary when the budget was so tight. The diet had to cater for a wide range of cultural and religious needs of prisoners, accommodate religious events like Ramadan, Passover and Sikh festivals and medical conditions like diabetes and coeliac intolerance.

The kitchen staff tried to make Christmas meals special, and were helped by a small increased budget of £2.10 per prisoner per day to work with. A typical Christmas menu included 'luxury' fish pie, a mushroom dish, half a roast chicken, sage stuffing, sausages, (halal, non halal and vegetarian), honey-roasted parsnips, carrots, Christmas pudding, Christmas muffins and a 'goody bag' containing non-alcoholic drinks and chocolate bars.

Catering for Ramadan was more complex, because it lasted a month. The fast meant Muslim prisoners did not eat or drink between dawn and sunset. During the summer sunset occurred well after the prisoners were locked up for the night and the kitchen had closed, so everything had to be prepared in advance and kept warm. One year insulated containers were bought for more than 400 Muslims. They didn't keep the food warm enough and were replaced at considerable cost the following year by an equal number of Thermos flasks. These kept the food warm but some prisoners put in complaints about the sameness of the menu. The prison jumped to attention and as a result Muslim chefs from three different cultural backgrounds were brought in to create more variety. The kitchen also had problems balancing the right number of meals for Ramadan with ordinary meals, particularly as some Muslims, either mistakenly or deliberately, also took a regular prison meal during the day.

One officer said: 'Some prisoners say they are fasting for Ramadan but then also demand lunch and the evening meal at 4.30pm and get furious when we stop giving them the second meal later for those who were fasting. Most of the Muslims are serious observers but about thirty per cent take the mickey and see it as an opportunity for getting extra food.' It was finally decided that those prisoners who ate during the day would only get their additional meals at the discretion of the imam.

- - - - - - - -

Added to these demands and problems was a constantly changing kitchen workforce that depended heavily on inmates, equipment that was often not fit for purpose and a permanent population of rats and mice. The kitchen was run by a senior prison officer and two industrial managers. From late 2014 changes were planned for only civilians to work in the kitchens. This was estimated to save the Prison Service about £11,000 a year per employee but with no officers on hand there could be no one in the kitchen trained to deal with violence.

The kitchen should have had thirty full-time working prisoners. In practice as few as twelve would sometimes turn up and the staff who worked there had no idea of the numbers in advance. Prisoners wore hygienic white hairnets, thin rubber gloves and were involved in all aspects of the catering. Kitchens are a high-risk area with plenty of knifes around and all prisoners were subjected to meticulous scrutiny before being allowed inside. It was one of the few jobs that gave prisoners the opportunity to work all day and earn more money than if they just worked mornings or afternoons.

Applicants were turned down if they had a history of drug abuse, were known traffickers, had sold contraband to other prisoners, or were bullies. Others didn't meet the educational standard required: as they had to be able to read the safety notices. Foreign national prisoners were rarely employed as they needed to understand and speak good English. It could take Security a month to clear a prisoner for work. Not surprisingly sometimes the paperwork got lost and the prisoner had to apply all over again. Or by the time he had been cleared he had been moved to another prison. Nor was it easy to employ people with experience of the catering industry to supervise the work, even though they apparently got more holidays and the hours were better than working in a hotel or restaurant. 'You get 35 days off a year in the civil service,' one manager told me. 'I think the civil service is one of the best employers to work for.' All these potential employees also had to go through stringent security checks.

Broken kitchen equipment was a continual problem. In theory there were sixteen ovens and six enormous vats. In practice I can't remember a time when all the ovens and vats were working properly at the same time. From 2006 onwards half the ovens and several boiling pans were usually out of action awaiting repair and remained so for months. It was an example of bureaucracy at its worst. All maintenance and repair work had to be recorded on Planet FM. It sounded like a radio station but was in fact a computerised system run by the National Offender Management Service (NOMS) for all prisons in the UK and Wales. No repairs, however minor, it even included replacing lightbulbs, could be carried out unless this was done. Once recorded, the work would then 'be assigned in accordance with their importance and urgency.'

This was the convoluted and time-consuming way of telling the prison works department to go ahead. It was also why unusable, sometimes enormous, pieces of machinery remained in the kitchen for years before they were removed. Getting rid of them wasn't seen as a priority. It also held up replacement parts and equipment. In May 2013 a Food Safety Management Assessment-Action Plan was completed by the prison. This highlighted that six boilers and four ovens weren't working. Nor were some lights. It also pointed out damaged doorframes and broken floor tiles near the vegetable preparation area.

It was left to a formal check a few months later by a senior Prison Service inspector and kitchen equipment supplier to highlight the real problems in the kitchen. Their report was scathing and stated that the equipment had not been properly used or looked after, that staff had carelessly allowed water to get into electronic parts of key cooking equipment, causing it to break down, that ovens were not being descaled, that mice had built nests in some of the equipment and had also eaten through the cables of cooking machinery and that general cleanliness was not up to scratch. The prison was told in no uncertain terms that no equipment would be replaced until there was evidence that the new equipment would not be treated as the old had been. Furthermore if there was just one case of food poisoning in the prison the kitchen would immediately be closed down.

Dealing with the rats and mice was a major headache. Apparently the introduction of feral cats had increased rather than decreased the problem as mice sought safety from the cats in the kitchen. It was a difficult job for the pest controller. It was common practice to put rat and mice poison in strategic places but this was not easy in Wormwood Scrubs for fear prisoners would steal the poison and use it for other purposes. Instead, a high-frequency device that the rats and mice allegedly disliked was tried.

— — — — — — — —

There was a four-week menu cycle and prisoners had to pre-select their choice from the national menu. The kitchen had to provide at least one hot meal a day and both lunch and dinner were prepared as much as possible the day before. Supplies came from a central authorised source; individual prisons were not allowed to seek out their own food bargains or buy from markets. Meat and fish arrived frozen, to be defrosted then kept in the fridge for cooking the next day. When I first became a monitor at Wormwood Scrubs prisoners had two hot meals a day. The five choices would include something with meat or fish, vegetarian, vegan and halal food with the possibility of kosher food on request. There was also always the option of rice instead of potatoes, a regular serving of curry, stew, pasta, chops, chicken and pies. In general prisoners liked sausages, chicken nuggets and pies. There was no specific mandate on how much fresh fruit or vegetables a prisoner had to eat, but attempts were made to provide an apple and occasionally a small side salad. There was strict portion control.

Prison officers came from their wings to the kitchen to collect lunch at 11am and dinner at around 4pm, for their specific inmates. They wheeled the food back on trollies to the hotplate in their wing. Prisoners then came down landing by landing so the numbers didn't get out of control to queue for food, which was served by fellow inmates. They subsequently took the plates back to eat in their cell. The servery was tucked away in the wing. It was cramped and a hot spot in many ways. Despite the presence of prison officers there were regular fights between prisoners as they jostled to get served. A survey on violence reduction revealed that prisoners felt less safe at the servery than anywhere else in the prison. Nor did the servers always keep to the strict portion control. Hotplate workers often dished out more than the basic portion to their favoured prisoners often to encourage them to do them favours. A lot of wheeler dealing and manipulation was known to go on. An officer said: 'Some prisoners see working at the servery as a business opportunity. They are not a great group of people in terms of responsibility.'

Nor did all the prisoners remember or care about sticking to their original choice and pointed to whatever they fancied from the selection available. Those who were called last to the hotplate regularly found their choice of meal had gone and what was left was meagre and unappetising. This caused much upset. One prisoner felt his punishment of being sent to the Segregation Unit for a fracas at the servery had been unfair: 'I took halal chicken because there was no ordinary chicken left. The officer stopped me, telling me I wasn't a Muslim. He then pushed me so I hit him. I have been sentenced four times from the ages of 15 to 24 and never once had a reason to hit an officer. But I couldn't bear that he was making a nuclear bomb event over a chicken leg.' It worked the other way round too. An officer said he had seen English prisoners grow a beard and refuse to eat pork, but then take non-halal chicken.

Many didn't care about healthy eating. I saw countless prisoners walk back to their cell with a meal that consisted of boiled potatoes and several slices of white bread. Bread was available slightly away from the hotplate and handed out by a couple of prisoners who also gave a green eating apple to those who wanted one. The apples, offered as an alternative to a cooked pudding and custard or a cake were not popular.

Prisoners had the opportunity to give their view of the food in a special complaints book and a monthly forum. They also complained to me. One was furious that a portion that used to consist of six chicken nuggets had now been cut to four. His anger increased when he allegedly discovered that 200 nuggets were left over at the end of lunch and had been thrown away. Something I was unable to confirm. 'It's not right that they won't give us second helpings,' he said. There were regular complaints that the boiled potatoes were 'rock-hard.' One prisoner was so 'disgusted' at the meals he issued an ultimatum. 'I want a Domino's pizza delivered or I will smash the cell up,' he threatened. He didn't get his way.

Another inmate was scathing about the food preparation. He wrote: 'The hygiene levels are poor beyond belief. It is 2011 not 1611. It is disgusting and poisnus (sic).'

There was also an opportunity for prisons to top up their diet, as well as buy toiletries, from the prison shop, known as Canteen. Goods were purchased from a London wholesaler and centrally stored at the Mount prison in Hertfordshire. Every week about 900 prisoners at Wormwood Scrubs bought about five items, spending on average about £12 each. Prisoners ticked off what they wanted from a long list of items and these were delivered a week later. If they forgot to fill in the form at the right time, they missed out. It happened a lot. The amount prisoners could spend was controlled by what category of prisoner they were and the money was taken out of their personal account. Items were more expensive than found in the average supermarket partly because containers made of glass couldn't be used and everything came in specially wrapped individual parcels. Favourite items were tobacco, crisps, tea, coffee, fruit juice, instant noodles and shower gel.

There were often arguments when prisoners were prevented from buying non food or certain toiletry items. One prisoner complained that he wasn't allowed to buy nail clippers. 'It doesn't make sense,' he said. 'When I go for education I have watched several prisoners take out part of a razorblade and use it to cut their toenails. You tell me if that is safer than a nail clipper.' I couldn't but did wonder how these prisoners had managed to conceal a potentially lethal razorblade when they were searched before leaving the wing and why they should want to cut their toenails in the classroom.

Delivering Canteen items to prisoners was also complex. The parcels were wheeled round the wings, and to prevent prisoners taking other prisoners' food by mistake or deliberately, everyone on the wing was locked up and staff delivered the individual items to the relevant cell door.

It was easy to find out what was popular from the wrapping thrown from windows on the wings. Not surprisingly there were countless mistakes, and many complaints about various items that hadn't arrived, some of which were totally justified. One prisoner put in a canteen order for £25 worth of goods. They arrived when he was in court. He was subsequently released but was still charged for the items. He got in touch with the prison but was merely told the order was signed for and delivered. Shortly afterwards he was back in the jail on another charge and tried again to get his money back. He could prove he was not in the prison on the day it was delivered but it still took many months before the money was finally correctly refunded.

CHAPTER ELEVEN
FOREIGN NATIONALS

Around forty per cent of prisoners at Wormwood Scrubs were foreign nationals. The numbers changed daily but in February 2014 there were 412 foreign nationals from 68 different countries. Some foreign nationals had committed crimes, others were held because they were suspected terrorists, illegal immigrants or a threat to the public. They were spread across the wings.

The largest group was Poles with 44 prisoners, followed by Romanians and Somalis. Less than a quarter of the foreign nationals had English as a first language and a considerable proportion barely spoke or understood it at all. Nor could many look forward to a release date. A significant number of these prisoners were totally confused about their rights, legal status and what would happen to them after their sentence. This was not surprising. Nothing about prison life was straightforward but the rules and procedures controlling foreign nationals was incredibly complex.

In 2009 the Home Office adopted an unpublished policy that stated that foreign nationals had to be detained at the end of their sentence under immigration act powers rather than be given their liberty for as long as it took to decide to remove them. The course of action was in response to adverse publicity in 2006 when it was discovered that more than a thousand foreign nationals had been released at the end of criminal sentences without being considered for deportation. It grew into a burning political issue. The policy was only discovered in 2011 when two foreign national criminals claimed they had been detained too long while the Home Office tried to remove them from the UK and their case finally went to the Supreme Court.

As a result, foreign national prisoners who had completed their sentence, were then renamed 'detainees', even if they had British citizenship, and stayed under lock and key, not knowing if or when they would be deported or released. The policy caused a furore and not just among human rights activists. Immigration removal centres were meanwhile bursting at the seams. Even if there had been space, the UK Border Agency (UKBA), the arm of the Home Office that deals with immigration and asylum, would not allow certain detainees-- including those convicted of sexual offences involving children, supplying or importing class A drugs, or those who would pose a serious risk to security--to go to the removal centres.

The fact was that Non-European Economic Area citizens sentenced to 12 months or more could be automatically deported when their sentences ended unless they could show that this would breach their rights under the Human Rights Act. While European Economic Area citizens - those in the EU plus Norway, Lichtenstein and Iceland - could also be deported on grounds of 'public policy, public security or public health.' Irish citizens could only be deported in exceptional circumstances.

It made life in jail difficult for both foreign national prisoners and staff, not least because many of the prisoners didn't appear to have been given the details of how the system worked. Many asked for a monitor to see them, although the majority preferred to speak to a man rather than a woman, to complain about their treatment. 'I am a British citizen,' many protested. 'But they are keeping me here and tell me I will be deported.' British citizenship didn't in itself prevent them from being deported, if they had not actually been born in Britain.

- - - - - - - -

Many did not understand, or had not been informed of how long they might have to wait. They initially thought that they would be deported within hours of completing their sentence. A regular cry was: 'I don't want to be in prison. I know I may be deported so please arrange for me to go to a detention centre NOW.' One prisoner struggled to express himself. 'I'm been hold under emmigration even know I'a British citizent I can proof.' (sic)

I tried to explain that even if there had been no mention of deportation when they were in court, once they had received a criminal sentence longer than a few weeks, their case was automatically referred to UKBA, which then considered whether to deport them. This would happen even if they had been granted indefinite leave to remain in the UK on asylum or family grounds. The number of foreign national prisoners in jail over the last ten years has more than doubled to represent over fourteen per cent of the total prison population in England and Wales.

Foreign nationals and detainees created a strange anomaly in Wormwood Scrubs. The prison, a designated local prison with a high turnover of inmates, wasn't tailored to suit the needs of long-term disgruntled foreign nationals who had served their time. There was also the added complication that detainees had different rights to criminals. It meant that as soon as they finished their sentence they had to be treated differently to regular prisoners. For example; they didn't have to share a cell with a sentenced prisoner and could wear their own clothing, like remand prisoners. Nor did they have to work, although if they wanted to they were supposed to be allowed to.

Until 2011 there was a foreign national coordinator in Wormwood Scrubs who could explain issues to these prisoners and help sort out their difficulties. The post disappeared because of cost-cutting and responsibility for foreign nationals was moved to the Diversity department. But this department was permanently short-staffed, the workload piled up so the job was split between various individuals at different levels of seniority. The result was less coordination. In addition statistics relating to foreign nationals were no longer thoroughly examined. Nor was their nationality always checked. The independent monitors felt this was far from satisfactory particularly as there were then around 500 foreign national prisoners in the prison out of a total of over about 1200 prisoners. Our concerns were included in our annual report of 2011-2012 to the Secretary of State.

In the mid-2000s we had been helped by a long-serving old-school member of staff who seemed to know all the foreign national prisoners by name, their problems and what stage their deportation had reached. He never looked up anything in a file but took pride in keeping the information in his head. Inevitably the increasing numbers of foreign nationals arriving in the prison meant this became an increasingly impossible task and he eventually took early retirement. A new Foreign National Coordinator was finally employed in February 2014. Independent monitors relied on foreign nationals approaching us to access help, but we remained unsure what percentage of them knew of our existence. They should have heard about the Independent Monitoring Board during the induction process shortly after they arrived at the prison. This information was available in 22 languages other than English. Understandably they might not have absorbed much as the first week or so in prison could be both a shock and confusing, particularly for those whose English wasn't good. The chaplaincy team also provided support to these prisoners, especially if they were from minority groups.

Their biggest problem was their lack of English, which was a huge barrier to understanding how the prison operated. The prison was full of leaflets and notices, but, to save money, most were not translated. The 2011 inspection of Wormwood Scrubs by the Chief Inspector of Prisons criticised this and stated: 'No other information or documentation apart from the induction was readily available in other languages and a number of foreign national prisoners said they generally did not know what was going on.' Some of the prison notices, often supplied by National Offender Management Service, were so strangely translated that even I struggled to understand what they meant. Even a variety of forms requesting attendance at Immigration Surgeries were in English, as were the prison rules. I often received surprisingly well-written applications, sometimes of a confidential nature, from a foreign national prisoner. But when I met the complainant on the wing I would find that it had been written for him by another prisoner who had since left the prison. Neither of us could understand the other. Sometimes I managed to find someone else who could translate. At other times there was no one available and it was difficult to help him.

One prisoner brought a fellow inmate to translate for him but didn't or wouldn't grasp the fact that prisoners don't decide when to leave a jail. His translated words were: 'I cannot return to my country for security reasons, and I can't stay in this prison. I must go home to my wife now as she cannot be in the house alone or come to prison. I have been here five weeks and that is enough. They put me in prison because they think I am a terrorist but I am not. I want to leave today.' Language problems also made it difficult for foreign national prisoners to apply for jobs, education and training as they had to pass a literacy test before they could work. Many thought this was discriminatory as most jobs did not require reading or writing. The literacy stipulation did, however, also affect English prisoners who could not read or write.

— — — — — — — —

It was also difficult to be accepted for a place in the Education department for prisoners whose first language was not English. They needed to complete a preliminary English language course first, but these had separate funding and were often not on offer. One officer thought it was wrong to give foreign nationals places in the Education department. 'They have done wrong and they should go. The courses and that includes learning English are a waste of time.' Without work or education foreign national prisoners spent a considerable amount of time isolated in their cells. Many drew attention to their plight by starting fires in their cells, self-harming or going on dirty protests. They would then end up in the Segregation Unit in solitary confinement, which didn't help their stress levels. It was also demanding on staff.

One depressed prisoner said: 'I tried to kill myself three times when I was at the immigration centre and now they put me in prison. My life doesn't have a future or any sense.' It was customary for those who committed serious offences in a detention centre to be moved to prison. Others threatened they would commit suicide if they were deported. Occasionally there would be an Imprisonment for Public Protection (IPP) when a prisoner would have to serve an indeterminate sentence. One of these prisoners was African and according to an officer 'rude and dismissive.' 'He won't engage with the anger management or violence reduction programmes,' I was told. 'We are only holding him until we can move him to a category A prison when a place becomes available.' Whenever an A category prisoner was in the jail security at Wormwood Scrubs went up several notches to conform with the more stringent standards of a top security prison.

Another concern for foreign nationals centred around phoning family and friends who lived in countries with different time zones. There was a system of free telephone credits for foreign nationals who didn't have any visitors come to see them, but these calls were confined to about two minutes. As there was no time limit on immigration detention, detainees could spend years locked up after they had completed their sentence waiting for their case to be resolved. In February 2014 the prison housed 46 detainees many of whom had been stuck for over a year. Both NOMS and UKBA were responsible for processing the necessary paperwork. In 2009-2010 ninety seven percent of investigations by the Prisons and Probation Ombudsman resulted in complaints against UKBA being upheld.

So little was clear cut and straightforward in the prison that no organisation or individual could automatically be blamed for deportation issues. But it certainly didn't help when foreign nationals refused to co-operate because they didn't want to leave the UK, especially if they had thrown away any ID as soon as they arrived in the UK. This enabled them to falsely claim to be a different nationality or refuse to reveal their country of birth. In addition administrative errors like an incorrect date of birth by just one number or a missed letter in a surname could, when performing a passport check, delay establishing a prisoner's nationality by months. Eventually illegal immigrants usually understood they would stay where they were unless they allowed themselves to be photographed and their fingerprints taken so their identity could be verified.

The situation was made worse by the severe national shortage of UKBA staff. A few UKBA staff operated from Wormwood Scrubs and concentrated on the prisoners within the jail. They were supposed to have one-to-one meetings with a prisoner and run regular immigration case surgeries for groups of prisoners, but the staff constantly changed and the workshops were discontinued not long after they had been set up due to prison officer shortages. It was also extremely difficult for foreign nationals to get any independent advice while they were in prison.

Officers' attitude to foreign national prisoners and detainees was mixed. One officer couldn't understand why foreign nationals were kept in London. 'It doesn't make sense to clog up London prisons. Most of them don't have families in London that would want to visit. They also need to be somewhere that can give them proper language support and any advice they need.'

Another experienced officer told me he believed that foreign nationals should automatically lose all their rights to stay in the UK once they had been found guilty of a criminal act. 'It's a decency factor,' he said. 'If you are a guest in another country you should behave yourself and not commit a crime. Otherwise it's time for tough treatment. Why should this country pay more than £30,000 a year to keep a foreign national in jail, when it would cost less than £1,000 to fly him home?'

He admitted there were, though, some advantages of having them in the jail. 'They keep a lid on potential trouble,' he agreed. 'If it wasn't for them we would most likely have more fights on the wing. Foreign nationals don't, as a rule, want to get involved in anything that could turn into mass rioting. Those who come from Eastern Europe, Asia and South America think Wormwood Scrubs is a hotel compared to the prisons in their own country. In South America, for example, prisoners tell me they would be ten to a cell. Nor can they believe they can have free education in jail. They think that if they got involved in disturbances within the prison they might have to serve whatever is left of their sentence in their home country, which most of them don't want to do.'

The official inspection of Wormwood Scrubs in 2011 seemed to confirm this. It noted: 'In our survey, foreign national prisoners, who made up 42% of prisoners, were more positive than those of British prisoners across almost all aspects of their treatment and experience at Wormwood Scrubs.'

Some detainees were willing to go home but UKBA was notoriously slow at dealing with casework especially if it involved complicated logistics. Decisions to deport were regularly made only a couple of days before the release date and arrangements for moving the prisoner sometimes appeared disorganised. On one memorable occasion UKBA sent movement orders to Wormwood Scrubs for the same prisoner to go to two different removal centres at the same time. The result was the prisoner remained where he was.

- - - - - - - -

It was also difficult to deport a foreign national when his country of origin refused to provide the necessary travel documents. Particularly uncooperative embassies included Somalia, Algeria, Iran and Angola. Prisoners only

knew for certain that they would be deported when an immigration detention order was sent to the prison and it was only then that they could talk to
a solicitor to see if they had grounds for appeal.

All flights back to their country of birth were paid for by the Home Office.
Ninety percent were scheduled flights. Some chartered flights were used,
for example to Nigeria and Ghana. Detainees had 72 hours notice if it was a
scheduled flight and five days if it was chartered.

Occasionally an individual prisoner was particularly difficult. One man
had apparently initially agreed to leave the UK but changed his mind at the
last minute once he was on the plane. He hit one of the security officers ac-
companying him and was taken off the flight. The next time attempts were
made to deport him he was accompanied by three security men and two
police officers. Despite this he created such a disturbance on the flight that
the captain of the plane decided to land in France soon after take off for
safety reasons. The prisoner subsequently claimed the security men and
police had assaulted him; they replied that all they were doing was trying to
restrain him. No one was sure of the next move for this particular prisoner,
but there was a possibility of a court hearing to decide if a restraint could be
used. The operation became very expensive.

There were other options for returning prisoners. The Ministry of Justice
operated an Early Removal Scheme that allowed the removal of prisoners
before their normal release date, so reducing the costs of keeping them in
prison and detention centres. It was not voluntary; all sentenced foreign national prisoners who had been given a fixed sentence and were confirmed by
UKBA as being liable for removal had to be considered under the scheme.

The Facilitated Return Scheme, which was often confused with the Early
Removal Scheme, was voluntary, and non-European foreign nationals could
apply for it. Those who were accepted and applied early in their sentence
could receive between £500 and a maximum of £1,500. Those who waited
until their sentence was over could receive up to a maximum of £750.

An officer told me that when the financial support from the facilitated
return scheme initially began in 2009 the maximum amount paid to prisoners was in the region of £3,000 and it was much easier for them to get at least
some of the money in cash. Subsequently more effort was made to ensure
the money was put to good use. Prisoners only received a small amount to
travel with and the rest came from a specific agency once they returned to
their country. As the money was intended to help them resettle, they also
had to provide a business plan before it was released. Even then it was not
in cash.

According to a Freedom of Information request, approximately thirty per cent of foreign national prisoners were removed under this facilitated return scheme in 2009 at an approximate cost of £6.3 million. The Ministry of Justice also estimated that, as a result of the early removal scheme, approximately 400 prison places in any given month would no longer be taken by foreign nationals, representing a saving of about £1.2 million a month.

CHAPTER TWELVE
GETTING BACK ON TRACK

Many prisoners were expelled or excluded from school. Nor have many held down a regular job. There was, in theory at least, a chance to do something about it in prison. Educationally, they had a lot of catching up to do but most offenders were easily distracted and showed little commitment. Half of the men in jails in England and Wales have no qualifications at all, and literacy skills below those of most 11-year-olds. To make learning more appealing, prisoners were paid about £1 to turn up for a morning or afternoon session that took place in the education block.

Because of the constantly changing population at Wormwood Scrubs it was difficult to achieve much, which was frustrating for both men and teachers. The standard of education on offer could also be poor. Education, like other aspects of prison life, was run in a target-driven, tick-box way, and certificates were handed out for almost nothing. Prisoners were so casual about turning up that one volunteer prisoner on each of the wings was asked to be 'education helper' and nudge prisoners to attend class. Despite this, many failed to materialise and attendance could fluctuate between 30%-80%. It didn't help that a prisoner could be on the verge of completing a short course but without warning be transferred to another jail where the same course was not available. I felt that, in preference to courses and certificates that would be worthless once the prisoner left jail, it would be more use long term for a local prison like Wormwood Scrubs to concentrate on helping prisoners develop personal skills.

The provider of the outsourced education in the Scrubs was A4E. It took over from Kensington and Chelsea College in November 2012 and operated in all London prisons. Ofsted, the educational watchdog, produced its first report on how A4E was doing in February 2013. On the positive side Ofsted acknowledged that its employability training helped prisoners into work at a higher rate than if they had no help, and that supportive and dedicated staff had good relationships with learners, helping them develop self-confidence and a range of employment skills. But basically found the provider inadequate. The report included the following: 'Too much teaching, learning and assessment is uninspiring or mechanistic. Performance in subject areas has rarely risen above satisfactory or requiring improvement in 10 years of inspection.' In addition Ofsted found that A4E's 'apprenticeship programmes have had consistently inadequate outcomes' and many prisoners left without their main qualification. Plus, 'Judgments, especially for learners' outcomes are too generous. The process for observing teaching, learning and assessment is not effective enough to drive up standards.'

Eight months later, in October 2013, Matthew Coffey, national director of further education and skills at Ofsted, talking at Wormwood Scrubs, underlined his concern and strongly criticised standards of education and training in all of England's prisons. He said it was unacceptable that not a single prison's education programme had been rated as outstanding over the past four years, and only one in three was judged to be good. He added that there would be a 'national outcry' if these figures related to state schools. The reality is that prisoners who are on the whole the most reluctant to learn need the best quality teaching.

Before prisoners could start any education programme they had to complete a test during their induction process shortly after they arrived at the prison. All prisoners were given the same low-level test regardless of whether they had left school with no qualifications or had a degree. The questions included the following:

Fill in the gap with the correctly spelt word from those in brackets.
We sat on the .... for a rest (grash, gras, grass, grase)
Underline the misspelt word and write the correct spelling.
My lucky number is severn
$5 + ? = 5$
$2p+2p+? = 5$
21, 24, 27, ?, 33
45p= £? (4.5, 450, 45, 0.45)

The education programme included language and numeracy, life and social skills, IT, preparation for work, developing parenting skills and introduction to journalism. There were also more practical courses like learning to be a barber, which was popular, gardening and food preparation. Someone in the education department came up with the idea of running a course in baking. The sum of £20,000 was spent on specialised equipment, but the project collapsed as there was no staff to run it. The equipment stood unused.

The main education block was risk assessed to take up to a maximum of 126 learners per session, nowhere near enough for a prison the size of Wormwood Scrubs. There were long waiting lists for some courses but so few of them concentrated during a lesson that I believed many prisoners turned up more for the money than anything else. Some prisoners felt it was too much like school, which they'd hated and didn't take it seriously. In the monitoring board's 2012-2013 Annual Report for the Secretary of State, we stated that students had too often been seen standing around, chatting or smoking rather than in the classroom. Fortunately prison staff stopped this and prisoners were subsequently only allowed to leave the class for one organised toilet break. Despite the negative aspects, some prisoners grasped the opportunity to learn. 'I think I've got a bit of sense on me now,' said one. 'Because of my past it's going to be difficult to get a job but I'm going to try to get an education.' Another bragged about his modest qualification but in doing so highlighted his extraordinary justification for being in jail. 'I already have an NVQ qualification for business studies,' he said proudly. 'I am here for violence not crime and shall carry on with my business interests.'

As the Coalition focused increasingly on rehabilitation and preparing prisoners for work, lack of space in the education department for the prisoners became more obvious. In 2013 education facilities spread to the wings and classrooms for up to ten prisoners were created. It was a small but important improvement. Some education support was initiated in the workshops and in the Segregation Unit.

Art and music were popular. 'Painting isn't like learning,' one prisoner said. 'It really relaxes me.' Art provided a creative outlet for a prisoner through which he could express himself, and could reveal more about how he felt than words alone. The charity The Koestler Trust, Art for Prisoners, which was located in the forecourt of the Scrubs, helped enable prisoners to find talents in themselves they didn't know they had. They organised an annual competition and also sold some of the prisoners' art work, with proceeds divided between the artist, the Trust and victim support.

I saw prisoners who were totally absorbed by creating something and very proud of the result. 'It's not bad, is it, Miss?' asked one prisoner showing me his self-portrait. 'Never thought I'd do something like this in a million years.' Its effect shouldn't be under estimated. His painting had given him a sense of self-worth, a valuable, elusive quality for inmates, and like gold dust in a prison. A prisoner who feels more positive about himself has taken a step, however tiny, that can lead to better behaviour in general and eventually perhaps a change in lifestyle.

There were no regular music lessons at the Scrubs but in March 2011, I attended a Modern Music Session run by the charity Music in Prisons. Two members of the charity came into the prison every day for a week, at the end of which eight prisoners combined to give a musical performance. The selected group were asked to write songs on the Monday to be performed five days later. The charity also provided instruments, including guitars and a drum set. The concert took place in the prison's Victorian chapel underneath painted crucifixes and saints who might well have stirred in their resting place at the volume of the music. The packed audience included prisoners, each one with an officer sitting next to him for security reasons, high-ranking governors, psychologists and me. Two of the prisoners wore prison uniform, the other six were in brightly coloured shirts. Seven original songs, largely rap, were performed, and the two instructors on guitar and piano helped kept the rhythm moving. The performers were easily as polished as a good boy band on The X Factor.

By the end the prisoners seemed overwhelmed both by what they had achieved and the audience's enthusiastic applause. It had been the first time any of them had come together in a co-operative exercise and they were amazed at how positive an experience it had been. It was genuinely moving. Each prisoner was awarded a certificate and then said a few words to the audience. A physically strong prisoner who had sung some rap tunes had tears in his eyes. 'Doing this has made me realise how many times I made my mum cry and how my being here affects my family,' he said. 'I don't want to come back.'

One of the charity workers added: 'We guided the inmates by taking their ideas and then helping them make them work. It was chaos in the beginning but slowly found its own rhythm. They also found respect for each other by working together and listening to each other.' He then turned to the prisoners and said: 'I hope you take these skills with you when you get out of jail.' A senior prison officer concluded the event by saying: 'I am very proud of the discipline and fantastic perseverance the men all showed. It was so well done.' One of the officers came up to me at the end to say she never would have believed it as most of the men were known to be difficult. It was an insight into what could be achieved, even for a few. Discussions were subsequently under way to see if the charity could come to the prison on a more regular basis.

The local authority ran a library service within the prison for use by prisoners. It had books and tapes in several languages and prisoners could borrow up to six books at a time. Although crime thrillers were the most popular, inmates liked books on sport and easy-to-read novels, such as those by Jeffrey Archer. There was also a collection of reference material for use in the library. The education department organised visits to the library. Prisoners could also attend once a week directly from the wing. Unfortunately a library visit always seemed to be the first thing that was cancelled whenever wings were short-staffed. It was very frustrating for prisoners who wanted to read to help pass the time spent in their cell. Prisoners would regularly contact me to complain that several weeks had passed without a library visit.

Another successful project was the Toe by Toe programme, which involved one prisoner helping another to read. Surprisingly some prisoners turned the opportunity down. For example, an Irish traveller who could neither read nor write, refused to take part. 'I am not interested,' he insisted. 'I didn't like learning in school, so why should I now? I am fine as I am.'

The well-equipped gym, with machines and weights, was always popular especially with the more muscular prisoners. Prisoners could take a course on Safe Lifting Techniques and learn how to be a personal trainer.

The prison also put on the occasional event. This included Black History Month, which was celebrated every October. Its aim was to remember significant people in the history of the African diaspora and highlight positive black contributions to British society. There was also a regular carol service just before Christmas.

－－－－－－－－

Learning a trade in prison has the potential to give prisoners an opportunity to change their lives, but in a local prison, due to the constant turnover of inmates, there was often not enough time to master the skills required. Remand prisoners could choose whether or not to attend a workshop. Convicted prisoners are supposed to work, unless they have psychological or other health problems or there is a security issue. Overall there were about 550 jobs available for 1200 or so inmates and more prisoners applied for work than there was work available. Pay varied between a modest 60p - £1.20 for a two-and-a-half hour morning or afternoon session. Many prisoners turned up because the money enabled them to make purchases, largely tobacco, from the prison shop, or because it helped pass the time.

The seven workshops offered low-grade often boring work that included how to clear litter with a pick-up tool and how to dismantle plastic headphones. Before offenders were allocated a job they had to attend a workshop to discuss the various options on offer. It was then left to the Central Allocations Team (CAT), to sort out who went to work in a workshop, on a wing and in the kitchen. The Security Department also had to give the OK to any placing. Prior to 2014 the allocation team had been called Local Employment

Office (LEO) and had a reputation for being slow and inefficient. In the mid-2000s it once lost a large pile of prisoners' applications for work places which caused considerable chaos and frustrated prisoners who wanted a job. For much of 2012 there was a two-month waiting list for prisoners to get a job, which ironically is the average time a prisoner spent in the jail. It was always confusing when the Prison Service altered the name of an aspect of prison life while fundamentally leaving it unchanged. I came to believe it was a way of papering over the deepening cracks in various aspects of the system. All the workshops operated with tight resources and regularly closed down, sometimes for months at a time, before reopening with something different on offer. Some had been structured badly for a local prison. The glass and glazing workshop, for example, ran a course that was too long and prisoners were often moved before they could get their NVQ certificate. There were also regular delays in getting supplies.

In 2011 preparations began for the sweeping changes in regime, the staff cutbacks and budget cuts that the Ministry of Justice announced would come into force in October 2013. The Coalition Government and NOMS stated they now wanted the focus of education, workshops and jobs to encourage prisoners in what was called 'purposeful activity' to increase their chances of finding jobs after they had been released. They believed that workshops were one of the key stepping stones for this to happen. It sounded like a no-nonsense, positive policy, but I believed it was basically unrealistic. Most prisoners didn't know or hadn't seen in their own family what a work ethic was, let alone have the discipline and enthusiasm to put it into practice. Time and again I saw several prisoners at what should have been the height of their purposeful activity in the workshops, lolling around chatting.

Several of the morning sessions even began with a long tea-break while one group sat in the painting and decorating workshop literally waiting for some paint to dry. Many prisoners also lacked the personal skills to recognise or grasp an opportunity when it stared them in the face. It would have been far more useful to go back to basics with prisoners and concentrate on life skills. I felt a motivation speaker coming in regularly for a few hours might have done more good than a weak course in a workshop. He could, for example, have tried to inspire offenders to want to get out of bed in the morning, be punctual, speak clearly and present themselves well at an interview. It could also have helped prisoners accept responsibility for what they did and cope rationally, rather than resort to violence, when they didn't get their own way. All of which would have been an important step towards taking control of their life.

This type of learning didn't, however, tick the right boxes in the prison's

Key Performance Targets (KPT) which prisons are measured by. When I first visited prison's workshops, they were largely run by keen prison officers who were dedicated to guiding and helping prisoners, and stayed in their job for years. They developed a strong relationship with inmates and prisoners often felt able to ask for advice on anything that bothered them. From about 2011 these jobs were largely outsourced with the assumption that the right choice of workshop would lead to more jobs outside. It was typical of NOMS' one-size-fits-all approach. There was evidence that prisoners who served a sentence of four years or more stood a reasonable chance of rehabilitation but it made little sense for those in the Scrubs.

It was also difficult to work out the thought process behind many of the decisions. For example, one of the workshops recycled waste, prisoners' boots, torn prisoners' clothing and broken furniture and in 2011/2012 apparently saved the prison £100,000. It was, however, closed down to make way for the expansion of the laundry. Roughly the same amount of money was then invested in an induction workshop. It took fourteen months to refurbish and seems to have been a flop.

When inductions were done in the First Night Centre all new or returning prisoners were given information about how Wormwood Scrubs operates at the same time. It was much more difficult to gather them together once they were spread round the wings as virtually all of them chose something else to do. The induction space was large enough to accommodate about fifty prisoners at a time, but on many days I was told as few as five prisoners turned up. As the induction took little more than about thirty minutes prisoners then hung around on the various sofas for a couple of hours until it was time to return to their wings. 'It's been a terrible waste of money' I was told by a member of staff. 'The induction was supposed to give prisoners purposeful activity but they do nothing here, whereas the recycling saved the prison a lot of money.' Another workshop was geared to help prisoners about to be released. This was more popular no doubt because it informed prisoners how to claim benefits and use resources like the Citizens Advice Bureau.

— — — — — — — —

Following Government policy on getting more prisoners into work in 2011 the prison laundry was given a £1.3 million refurbishment. This was to enable it to take on contracts and bring much-needed funds into the prison. The laundry had a positive atmosphere. Prisoners could earn up to £15 a week if they worked all day. They were kept busy and could see they were doing necessary work. Although at times it was uncomfortably hot there was good camaraderie between staff and officers. Almost simultaneously, however, the laundry was plagued by shortages of staff that not only delayed prisoners being trained but also stopped outside contract negotiations from moving forward because delivery dates couldn't be guaranteed. I was told it had become 'a shambles.'

Officers regularly told me the workshops were largely a waste of time. 'There is a lot of pretence going on that attending a workshop will help prisoners find jobs when they get out,' one knowledgeable officer insisted. 'It's nonsense because most employers are very prejudiced against anyone with a criminal record and if they got anything the chances are it would be poorly paid. What needs to happen first is to encourage these men to think entirely differently, meet different people and see that there is another way of life.'

Although prisoners weren't necessarily keen on work, they kept a close eye on their payments, which were made into their personal prison account. There were many applications to the monitors about missed or incorrect amounts. It was one of the more straightforward problems we dealt with. They also asked for help when they were refused or lost their prison jobs. 'I really want to work in Reception,' one wrote. 'But Security say I am too risky and won't let me. I don't know what the problem is. I have been out of prison for years. Do you think it might be because in the past I've been sentenced for firearm offences?'

Another prisoner with several gold teeth told me he'd take a job anywhere. 'Every time I put in for something they tell me I am a security risk. Being in my cell all the time is frying my brain. Can't you do something? I need a job to get into the rhythm of having a job so I'm rehabilitated when I go out.' I told him it was impossible to negotiate with Security on these matters.

Another prisoner claimed he had been dismissed from serving meals because he had given a prisoner two extra potatoes. I checked. He had been in trouble several times before and had received warnings. Portion control was considered to be important. This had been his last chance and he was found not to have performed his duties 'to the required standard.'

Attendance at the workshops was erratic and varied between 40% and 70%, depending on the workshop and other things the prisoner might choose to do, for example go on a legal visit or a medical appointment. Stickability was not their strong point. The workshops didn't keep a reserve list of prisoners. This was partly because they didn't know who would show up until the session started, by which time, if they were short on numbers, it was impossible to get an officer to go back to various wings to bring replacement prisoners along. It was also because there was no centralised allocation system to help staff in the wings get prisoners to the right place at the right time or enable them to sort out clashes in advance.

In an effort to provide more jobs for prisoners, in 2012 attendance at the workshops, but excluding the kitchen or laundry, was split so that prisoners attended half a day rather than a full day. It also cut prisoners' earnings in half. As most jobs on the outside require a full day's attendance I didn't think this did much to establish a prisoner's work ethic.

This dramatic change seemed not to have been taken on board by the subsequent Prison Service Public Sector Benchmark Project for Wormwood Scrubs. Dated February 2013, which was several months after a prisoner's working day was cut in half, it nonetheless maintained its intention 'to make prisons places of real work, where prisoners acquire a work ethic working as close to a normal working week as possible and acquire skills and experiences which will best equip them to obtain and keep a job on release. This signals a significant shift away from regimes in which education and vocational training could dominate and towards a regime where, important though both those regime components are, they complement a greater emphasis on work itself. The approach at Wormwood Scrubs has therefore been to focus on enabling prisoners to acquire 'job ready' skills – the habit of going to work routinely and behaving well – and experience in work what they are most likely to find in the communities in which they will live on release. We have therefore sought to identify work to enhance the regime which is 'job market relevant.' ' The reality was very different from the theory. Unfortunately worse was to come.

It is important to acknowledge that there were some tiny green shoots that might at least have encouraged a broader way of thinking. Useful information was available through the prison's Job Centre Plus workshop where offenders could get information about the voluntary agencies that could help prepare them for life after prison. St. Mungo's charity gave information on housing, although not necessarily an actual place to live. Prisoners could discover where to go for up to date information on training, employment, financial advice, a counselling service and how to claim state benefits. They also heard how they could work for the local community on local, environment or sports projects, with the elderly or disabled, and how this could help them build self-confidence and develop a sense of social responsibility.

Wormwood Scrubs also developed links with eight London boroughs to support prisoners who had been sentenced to less than twelve months in custody, who had no statutory post-release support and were most likely to fall through any rehabilitation net. These included London Probation Trust, Metropolitan Police, the local authority, voluntary sector organisations, faith-based organisations and a few local businesses. The Chaplaincy at Wormwood Scrubs also developed a through-the-gate mentoring service for prisoners leaving jail. They began training volunteer mentors of all faiths and none. The aim was to meet regularly with their mentee for three months before his release, meet him at the gate on the day of his release and continue to support him emotionally and in practical ways once he was back in the community.

By February 2013 they had recruited 50 mentors to help 30 prisoners. Unfortunately in practice the mentor only had about four weeks rather than three months to build up a relationship with his mentee, which I was told was not enough time for loyalty to develop. As a result the prisoner often didn't bother to contact his mentor once he had left jail. Some mentors dropped out too because they thought the prison was too inflexible about vetting them. Instead they had to take several days off work to go through all the necessary procedures even before they had met the prisoner they were hoping to help.

Rehabilitating prisoners was difficult and complex. Somewhere on the arduous journey from a life of crime to being a law abiding citizen an offender had to reach a tipping point when a combination of elements made him feel able to put his past behind him for good. If he also had mental health, or drug issues or had only served short sentences in prison his conversion would be even more problematical.

A plethora of statistics highlighted the immense difficulties for offenders to get back on track. A survey by the Chartered Institute of Personnel and Development showed that people with a criminal record were amongst those that 60% of employers deliberately excluded when recruiting and that almost one quarter of employers would not consider employing a homeless person.

The Revolving Doors Agency found that 49% of prisoners with mental health problems had no fixed address on leaving prison. Of those who had a secure tenancy before going to prison, 40% lost it on release. Home Office research found that prisoners who had accommodation arranged on release were four times more likely to have employment, education or training arranged than those who did not.

The Prison Reform Trust stated that about 30% of people released from prison would have nowhere to live: that people serving short prison sentences were 58% more likely to be reconvicted within the first year of leaving prison and two to three times more likely to reoffend if they did not have suitable housing: 75% of prisoners suffered from mental disorders and alcohol or drug problems; 35% of young people aged 16 – 25 felt a lack of accommodation was the factor most likely to make them reoffend. Prisoners who had problems with both employment and accommodation when they were released from prison had a reoffending rate of 74% during the year after custody, compared to 43% for those with no problems. In 2011-12, just 27% of prisoners entered employment on release from prison. A survey of prison outreach services run by Citizens Advice, discovered that debt was one of the top five issues that could cause reoffending or poor reintegration into society. There was also the practical issue that many prisoners languished in the dark ages before computers.

The combination made spending time in the right workshop or getting an NVQ qualification pale into insignificance by comparison.

CHAPTER THIRTEEN
LOST PROPERTY

Issues over prisoners' property kept monitors almost as busy as dealing with prisoners who complained about their health. Private possessions were lost all the time: between prisoners leaving court and arriving at the prison, when they were transferred between prisons, and within the prison. It seemed to have a very low priority within the prison service, but a high one in a prisoner's life. Trying to track lost items, some of which were valuable, was sometimes an incredibly lengthy business.

How property was handled provided another example of the chaotic antiquated ways in which prisons sometimes have to operate. For example, the details of a prisoner's property were recorded by hand. There was no central inter-prison record. Nor, for budgetary reasons, were there any plans to computerise the system, although this would make a huge difference. It would be easy to see exactly what was on a list that could also follow a prisoner electronically if he moved prisons.

Instead, the forms were completed by hand, sometimes in a scrawl, on four different coloured sheets of papers to identify what type of property it was. If it was stored in the prison's cavernous property department – it was known as 'stored property' – if it could stay in the prisoner's cell it was called 'in possession' property.

The routine was that when prisoners arrived at Reception their property was handed over by Serco to the Reception staff. Because of overcrowded vans, the amount a prisoner could take was limited to 15kg per person. Excess property was stored at the National Distribution Centre in Branston, near Burton-on-Trent, which was often full to overflowing and difficult to get anything out of. The property handover occurred when staff were at their busiest and rarely had time to check all the items against the list Serco provided. Prisoners were not allowed to keep cash and any money they had was handed over. It went into the prisoner's named account but was under the Governor's control. Many of the prisoners were traumatised at finding themselves in a prison, especially if it was for the first time and they had arrived late and hungry, and didn't take the opportunity to check that the property record was correct.

The arrangement was that prisoners could claim compensation for stored property that went missing, while the 'in possession' property was their responsibility. This led to all sorts of issues when prisoners went to court, as sometimes through ignorance, or because they couldn't be bothered to pack it up, items would be left behind. Prisoners were not always returned to the same jail and once it was known a cell had been vacated it was cleared for the next inmate and the lot could disappear. Even within the prison it could take several days to get property moved from the property department to a wing or from one wing to another. It was best if a prisoner stuffed everything in a see-through plastic bag and carried it with him.

Prisoners would complain, and when they didn't get a satisfactory answer, which was often, they would ask a monitor for help. 'Where is my prayer mat?' one Muslim prisoner wrote. 'I have been waiting for it for over three weeks. Also my Koran, which is something for me to read.' 'Please,' wrote another. 'I need to get some important documents from the property department. Otherwise I am going to be homeless.'

Sometimes it was difficult to know if a prisoner was telling the truth about items he claimed were lost, particularly as many of them seemed to buy top-of-the-range items just before they found themselves in jail. I received many complaints that their 'brand new' St Laurent/Hugo Boss/Armani/Ted Baker jeans/jackets, 'brand new' Nike/Adidas trainers, the latest PlayStation, and gold watches allegedly worth between £4,000 and £10,000, had gone missing.

It turned out that the £10,000 gold watch was a genuine loss and the prisoner was finally offered decent compensation but only once he had appealed to the Prisons and Probation Ombudsman.

- - - - - - - -

The process for claiming compensation was long-winded. Naturally, full details were required about the item allegedly lost and its value, but the prison, understandably in some but not all cases, always seemed to drag its feet. This meant that the prisoner had to be particularly tenacious. Compensation came directly out of the prison's own budget. Even when the prisoner proved his case, a year could go by before money changed hands. I know of several cases where prisoners repeatedly submitted complaints, or asked monitors to do so on their behalf.

Property left at other prisons could take a long time to recover, for a variety of reasons that were not always the prisoner's fault. Individual prisons had to pay for property to be transferred to another prison from their budget. This was expensive for just one prisoner, especially if the distance was significant. So the prisoner had to wait, often for months, until there were other prisoners in the same situation close by. While some officers were valiant in their attempts to retrieve a prisoner's property, others did the minimum. One prisoner, for example, had waited weeks for his property to arrive from a detention centre. He put in a complaint and received a reply that the centre claimed it had sent it. Wormwood Scrubs, however, did not receive it. There was no helpful suggestion of what he or the prison could do next and despite some efforts by monitors unfortunately the property was never found.

Valuable property caused a particular problem. Staff were not allowed to identify jewellery as gold or silver as they were not experts. Instead, it was described as 'yellow' or 'white metal'. Larger items were sealed in a bag and stored while small items were put in a safe. Following a spate of thefts from the Property Department in 2010, when some storage bags were found ripped open and emptied, suspicion fell on prison staff and CCTV was installed close to the area where the small items were stored. However, film footage was only kept for two weeks even though the theft might not become obvious for months when the prisoner was released.

If prisoners failed to take all their property with them when they were released, it was kept in the prison or at Branston for twelve months. It would then be destroyed. Curiously, some prisoners would wait until they came back to Wormwood Scrubs, sometimes years later, before checking on their property and then complaining to us that it was missing.

CHAPTER FOURTEEN
ALL CHANGE

At the height of the recession in 2010 the Prison Service announced a comprehensive spending review. This included 20% of cuts in frontline prisons, probation and court staff. The Governor of Wormwood Scrubs told the Independent Monitoring Board that the prison had to save £1.34 million by the end of the year. It was the start of savage cutbacks of both staff and budget, timed to come to fruition in October 2013 and would lead to the biggest changes in the way prisons were run in over 100 years. The Government talked about rehabilitation and giving prisoners a good work ethic that would in turn reduce reoffending, but from my monitor's perspective it seemed unlikely that this could be possible when simultaneously Wormwood Scrubs' budget was to be cut by 21%. This amounted to about £4.9million. Staff numbers, which were already quite tight at a total of 585, would be reduced by 128.

The three new policies were given the titles Fair and Sustainable, Benchmarking and New Ways of Working, and followed each other in such quick succession that there was little time for any of them to bed in. It left many staff reeling. 'We will be down to minimum staffing levels every day,' said one. 'We won't be able to cope and I don't think we could guarantee the safety of prisoners.' 'The pace has been so challenging,' added another. 'It is the most difficult and pressurised time I have experienced in the last thirty years.'

Fair and Sustainable, a brainchild of NOMS, was a new, very complicated eleven-band staff structure with a three-tier pay arrangement. Benchmarking, a way of judging standards against best practice in the competitive market, was intended to 'refresh' public prisons by making them more efficient and help reduce reoffending. New Ways of Working was the application of Benchmarking in practice and meant that staff had to work harder and be more flexible. It also changed their job titles and roles.

Some senior prison staff thought the sweeping changes and financial restrictions were intended to stave off privatisation. I was told: 'We have to do it, as that is where the benchmark is and what the private sector is doing. If they can do it, we can't say we won't. Otherwise there will only be a rump of public service prisons left.' If that was the case then many prisoners and officers were given an exceedingly tough time because of the overriding desire not to be part of the private sector.

Others felt the prison was being knocked into a different shape precisely in order to make it more suitable for privatisation. 'Though,' added a staff member, 'I am not certain whether the private sector is necessarily inherently better. Some private sector establishments are experiencing severe difficulties.' Oakwood, a vast private prison near Wolverhampton run by G4S, opened in 2012 and was meant to be the blueprint for future prisons, a position that was oddly unaffected by the fact that it was not only given the lowest performance rating possible by the Ministry of Justice but was also the scene of a major riot in January 2014. Staff at the Scrubs were not surprised. 'The company put in a very cheap bid to run it and it was obvious that it would explode in time,' an officer told me. 'I don't think it is either ethical or moral to run a prison to make a profit.'

The reality was that £2.4 billion was allocated every year by the Ministry of Justice for NOMS effectively to rehabilitate offenders and cut crime. But, despite this huge outlay, reoffending rates remained stubbornly high, with half or more of offenders committing crimes within a year of release from prison. Something drastic had to be done.

- - - - - - - -

Meanwhile, the Prison Officers Association said assaults on staff and inmates in jails across the UK rose from 13,804 in 2011 to 14,858 in 2012, including about eight a day on officers. The POA warned that this was likely to get worse because of budget cuts and job losses. By 2012 these unprecedented cuts were putting such pressure on the jail that was already overstretched that the IMB's Annual Report of June 2012-May 2013 for the Justice Secretary that I wrote with input from board members stated:

'The Board's concerns over the safety of both prisoners and staff have significantly increased over the reporting year. The Governor and his staff have done their best in increasingly difficult and demanding circumstances. But the Board now believes that delivering a regime in Wormwood Scrubs that is safe, decent and secure is being seriously compromised both by staff who are stretched to breaking point and stringent financial restraints. There are insufficient staff or resources and this has had an impact throughout the prison.'

It continued: 'It has fuelled the Board's belief that the prison is on a knife-edge. Staff have resorted to the use of force or control and restraint measures to control prisoners by an alarming 49 % more in the first six months of 2013 as compared to the same period in 2012.'

The Board's view, and we are supposed to be the Ministry of Justice's eyes and ears, that the prison was on a knife edge was rejected by a variety of Prison Service employees and by letter from Jeremy Wright, Minister of Justice. However, I maintain that the public has a right to know the findings of my own unique experience as an independent monitor over a decade, and what several governors and long-serving officers said all along: that the new regime, along with the drastic cutbacks wouldn't work and there was a chasm between governmental theory and what happens in practice. This view was endorsed by the Chief Inspector of Prisons on BBC Radio 4's Today programme in June 2014 when he expressed his concern about the 'extremely serious' state of prisons.

In September 2013, a month before the new regime started Michael Spurr, Chief Executive of NOMS, declared: 'Our more efficient national model for running safe and secure prisons is being introduced at Wormwood Scrubs next month. This will help maximise opportunities for rehabilitation, with more prisoners engaging in full-time work, while staff will be deployed efficiently so a positive regime is routinely and consistently delivered.' The reality was very different. A long-service officer commented: 'What we are being told is what they want us to believe. It is just not true.'

In fact the start of the new regime on 15 October 2013 was chaotic. Officers of all ranks, who had been used to spending years on the same wing, were overnight expected to have a 'flexi-day', become troubleshooters and go wherever they were needed. It left the senior officers, some of whom were in charge of a particular wing for the first time, with no idea early that morning how many staff they would have, who they would be, or how long they would stay on the wing. The powers that be also decided that this was the day to make significant changes to the food prisoners were given.

As Chair of the monitoring board I went in to observe how the changeovers were working. One wing was expected to run with five staff for more than 200 prisoners: six months previously there had been twelve. Fortunately officers have it in their DNA to think of safety first and foremost both for prisoners and themselves with the result that prisoners were kept locked in their cells.

Mostly they stayed there all day. This meant they didn't go for either educational courses or workshops. Prisoners' pay, however, was not stopped as it wasn't their fault they couldn't go to work, a decision that quite possibly stopped a riot. There were not enough staff to take prisoners to have visits. Instead, many friends and family were turned away at the gates, even though some had travelled long distances with small children. Very few if any prisoners were taken for their medical appointments. One wing managed to give out the morning dose of methadone to over a hundred drug addicts but with so few officers to lock and unlock cells it took more than two hours when it was usually done in one. This negatively affected other aspects of wing routine. There weren't enough officers to let the prisoners out to collect their lunch, even one landing at a time, so senior governors and administrative staff were urgently summoned from other parts of the prison and rushed over to help. The governors served the meal, while the admin staff, some of whom had never worked with prisoners before, let alone on a wing, stood around in their uniforms to give prisoners the impression everything was under control.

These were not just the first day's teething troubles. Weeks later almost all areas of the prison were in turmoil. It was obvious that the staff had been so reduced that, despite their best efforts and the governors working all hours, they couldn't run the prison according to the statutory orders. 'I am not told until 7.30am on the day who will be working on my wing,' said one senior officer. This was crucial information because, while the basic prison routine operated across the board, each wing had its own characteristics, demands and needs.

To respond to the acute lack of staff, some extra officers were rushed in from Downview Prison in Sutton, Surrey, on a temporary basis. One wing was staffed several times with officers who had never set foot in it before. A monthly wing report subsequently recorded that 'when there is no continuity the wing does not run as well and prisoners can be more aggressive.'

Instead, many staff had to work in three different parts of the prison a day. At one level it made sense to take officers from quieter areas to more hectic ones. Reception, for instance, was often frantic in the early morning when prisoners were released or went to court and again in late afternoon when new prisoners arrived from court, but was quieter during the day so staff could be spared. But in practice it was tough to work flat out all day in different often stressful and frantically busy areas of the prison with no time to get a proper briefing. Staff, I was told, could no longer expect to begin and end their shift working on the same wing. When there was down time they had mountains of paperwork to deal with. It was again unrealistic to expect them to manage both. And so it proved. Staff stress levels shot up, some took sick leave, leaving those who were left with fewer staff to manage even more work. On one day in December 2013 nineteen officers were on sick leave; a few days later the number had reached 26.

'It's hard to cope now staff have been cut to the bone,' one officer said. 'Just one officer off sick makes a huge difference to the running of a wing.'

Life was always difficult at the coalface of a prison. Criminals could be violent, mentally ill, unpredictable, volatile, suicidal, manipulative and looking for a chance to escape. Officers knew this and needed to stay wary and alert at all times and particularly when inmates knew the wings weren't functioning as they should. The stress level remained high.

Management had also assumed, incorrectly it turned out, that officers would gladly volunteer to do overtime, known as Payment Plus, possibly up to their working limit of 52 hours a week. In reality few took it up. 'Most of us were just too tired after the hectic shifts,' I was told. Instead, a regime began of locking up prisoners on the top two landings of a wing for half the day and those on the lower two landings for the latter half. It was called Uptime Downtime, and meant prisoners in theory could go to education or workshops during the half day they were unlocked.

— — — — — — — —

Meanwhile the lack of updated and accurate paperwork affected those new to a wing. One officer commented: 'I am going to wings where the names of prisoners have been spelt incorrectly or differently in two different places and documents don't correspond. I didn't know for sure who was or wasn't in the wing at any particular time. If you can't get the roll call right you can't let staff go home at the end of their shift. I have been on a wing when I didn't know if I had 65 or 84 prisoners on a landing.'

It is important to state yet again that the staff and regime changes were forced on the prison by NOMS. The chaos was not the staff's fault. Long-serving governors tried to argue that the changes would never work, that they were too drastic and that the safety of the prison would be at risk, but their advice was in the end disregarded. While the changes may work in some prisons, at Wormwood Scrubs they were a disaster in their original form. Nor was it merely teething troubles.

When there weren't enough staff prisoners were automatically locked in their cells. Apart from a stipulated exercise time of thirty minutes, there was no statutory limit to the amount of time they could be confined to their cells and many were locked up 23 hours out of 24. Understandably, prisoners didn't respond well to being in their cells up all day. When they came out to collect their lunchtime meal they didn't want to go straight back, became aggressive and shouted at officers. Many of the staff admitted they felt scared. 'How can we keep prisoners safe if we don't feel safe ourselves?' asked one.

Another added: 'I have been here twenty years and it's only now that I feel unsafe. Staff are supporting each other but it is not enough. I am very alive to the increased risk of trouble. As soon as there is a difficult situation and there are many more of them, I automatically think 'where is my back-up if I need it?' but there isn't any. You are not going to tackle a prisoner who is behaving badly by yourself because you could get seriously physically assaulted. '

One senior officer confided: 'I fear the prison will operate with significant shutdowns from now to eternity. There is absolutely no room for slack. Morale is very low. We are even having to rely on decent older prisoners to keep the younger ones under control and avoid riots.'

I was in a wing one lunchtime when a prisoner who was queuing for his meal recognised I was a monitor and rushed over to me. As he voiced his complaints, others left the queue and joined him. Their anger was palpable and I was quickly surrounded by at least twelve very angry prisoners. I told them I understood they didn't want to be locked up all day and that the food was awful and would take their names and numbers and report their concerns to a governor. Then a senior officer rushed over to me. 'You are holding back the prisoners from getting their meals,' she snapped, as if I was one of the inmates. 'You are slowing everything up. I can't let more than a few out at any time.'

I didn't take it personally as an important part of my role was to check that prisoners were being treated humanely and fairly. It was also obvious she was genuinely worried that this small group of complaining defectors could ignite trouble. It was astonishing bad timing that major changes to meals were happening at the same time as the change in staffing levels and regime. Instead of having two proper meals a day prisoners would only have one. From October 2013 lunch would always be cold. This means nothing in the world outside, and a great many people have a sandwich at lunchtime. But a change in routine, especially if it related to food, was a shock to prisoners, many of whom were like simmering volcanoes. I moved to the server to look at the food and it seemed as if portion sizes had been significantly cut. The new-look lunch consisted of a small soft plain baguette, with a side choice of a cigarette-packet-sized portion of corned beef, or some peanut butter, plus the most unappetising egg-cup size portion of mixed pulses. One prisoner said dismissively: 'It wouldn't be enough for my four-year-old.' Another asked why he couldn't have any butter. It looked more like wartime rations and bore little resemblance to the suggested menus found in the mandatory prison service order for feeding prisoners.

The 4.30pm hot meal was little better. During the early weeks of the regime wings sometimes ran out of food before everyone was fed, or the food was cold, or the choices weren't available. Resentful locked-up prisoners kicked their doors in anger and frustration and the level of self-harming went up. After a few weeks it was obvious that the meagre lunch was threatening the stability of the prison. A senior governor suggested that the baguette be filled with either the corned beef, peanut butter or ham in the kitchen, rather than being served separately, to make it appear more appetizing and that a packet of crisps, an apple and instant noodles should be added to bulk up the food. Orders were given for the imposed tight budget to be temporarily ignored. Ironically the cold lunch made a considerable dent in the budgeted cuts. 'It will cost an extra £57,000 a year because of all the packaging needed,' I was told.

— — — — — — — —

As the weeks went by the amount of contradictory information I received as Chair mounted up. It was difficult to know whether the conflicting information was due to the general chaos or a decision to keep anything that reflected badly on the new regime as quiet as possible. I was told by some officers that whole wings had been shut down for days. Other governors denied this and because there was so little time to deal with administration, it was difficult to find written evidence of whether they had been closed down or not. I heard that three out of five wings had been locked down for the entire day, although one managed to open for an hour in the evening, that the fourth was shut down in the morning and the fifth during the afternoon. This too was denied. I was also told that as well as arranged lockdowns, which officers were trying to work round, there would be spontaneous lockdowns they weren't told about in advance. These made planning any sort of routine in a wing very difficult.

Efforts were made to get prisoners to workshops and education but on one day because of the lockdown only 39 students out of several hundred turned up at education. The empty classes upset the teachers. Many prisoners were rejecting the opportunity to learn as they had been told they had to choose between going to education or having a shower, but couldn't be let out of their cells to do both. Some decided to stay put on the wing, be clean, and perhaps also get the chance to phone their family. Others chose to miss out on the showers. After a week or so this resulted in a complaint from the teaching staff to management that the smell emanating from some of the men had become very unpleasant. Even those prisoners who chose to work or go to education regularly arrived late. They could only go in supervised groups and as the wings were so short-staffed all the necessary preparations took much longer. Time and again I saw prisoners standing around for about an hour waiting for the wing gates to be opened so they could go on their way. Since rehabilitation and getting prisoners prepared for work when they left jail was a key government target, this did not reinforce the importance of being punctual. It also meant the educational or work session lasted much less than its allotted time. I was told: 'Afternoon prisoners should arrive at the education department by 1.45pm, but are now not often here until 3pm. We just can't get through the same amount of work.'

The reality could hardly be more different to what was wanted. The aim of the Prison Service Public Sector Benchmark Project in February 2013 to "identify work to enhance the regime and make it job market relevant" was also failing.

The laundry, for example, could have been the one area of the prison that was 'job market relevant' and stood a genuine chance of equipping prisoners to cope in the world outside, but it suffered enormously from the lockdowns and chronic shortage of staff. At times not even the prison kit could be washed and on one occasion I was told that prisoners had to wear the same clothes for two weeks before clean kit was available. Crucially, the laundry had to relinquish contracts with commercial organisations that it had been so hoping to get. 'We can't run external laundry contracts if the laundry keeps on being closed for lack of staff who supervise the work and prisoners who are locked up. We had several interested parties but understandably they want guaranteed delivery.' The laundry was intended to be the jewel in the prison's efforts to move significantly forward with rehabilitating prisoners. Instead it was emasculated before it even got going, and the sixty jobs it was supposed to provide for prisoners shrunk to a maximum of thirty.

The staff shortages were felt throughout the prison. Officers in quieter departments like property were whisked away so often to support colleagues facing difficulties on the wings that they had no time to do their real job. As a result there was a six-to-eight-week delay before new prisoners could access any of their property. This also included important paperwork relevant to their trial that they were entitled to have in their cells.

Officers on the wings had no time to deal with prisoners' issues including complaints. This too seemed to fly in the face of specific Prison Service instructions. A Prison Service order dated February 2012, less than eighteen months before the regime was changed, dealt with prisoners' complaints. It stated: 'An effective system for dealing with prisoner complaints underpins much of prison life. It helps to ensure that the Prison Service meets its obligation of dealing fairly, openly and humanely with prisoners. It also helps staff by instilling in prisoners greater confidence that their needs and welfare are being looked after, reducing tension and promoting better relations. A prison's equilibrium is more likely to be maintained if prisoners feel they have an accessible and effective means of making a complaint, an outlet for their grievances and confidence that their complaints will be considered properly, with reasons given for decisions.'

It continued: 'The three-day target for replies (to complaints) is abolished in favour of a flexible target that reflects the urgency of the individual case. However, prisoners must receive a response within a maximum of five working days but an interim reply can be regarded as meeting this target. Nevertheless, a full reply must be given in the shortest period possible.'

From my experience this this didn't happen. While some prisoners received a vague holding note, most waited weeks to get an answer to their complaints, turning in the meantime to the independent monitors. Our green metal box was packed with applications from prisoners who wanted answers to issues that ranged from how they could get hold of their property to the lack and poor quality of the food. One prisoner, however, had an original complaint: 'I am not getting my newspaper until 7pm in the evening by which time it is yesterday's news. Some days I don't get it at all.'

Many of the applications sent to the monitors verged on the desperate. 'We are now living like animals but without any exercise,' wrote one man. 'I have been to many jails but never one with a regime like this. We are locked up at least 23 hours every day with no fresh air and even the windows in the cell are small. I know we are all criminals but even criminals have certain rights. Could I please ask too that you do something about the food.' Shortly afterwards, a petition from over fifty prisoners was handed in about the poor food. The fact that they got it together was an achievement in itself.

—————————

Other changes included a ban on prisoners receiving books. This, I was told, included course work books from the Open University for a couple of bright prisoners who wanted to do a degree. A teacher in the Education Department said many months were lost while they tried to work a way round the system to get the books to the prisoner. It could well have been due to staff shortages. Even though only two prisoners were affected, it undermined their opportunity for effective rehabilitation. Other changes affected the way prisoners were graded. Changes to the Incentives and Earned Privileges (IEP) scheme were announced in April 2013 and introduced on 1 November 2013. These made it harder for prisoners to be upgraded but easier for them to be downgraded. Prisoners were expected to 'demonstrate a commitment towards their rehabilitation' by engaging in purposeful activity, behaving well and helping other prisoners. No obvious allowance was made for how difficult this would be if you are locked up in your cell nearly all day.

The Chief Inspector of Prisons highlighted the fact that purposeful activity in prisons had 'plummeted' during 2013 with the Inspectorate reporting the worst outcomes for six years.

During the first three frenzied months of the new regime there were several potentially dangerous incidents. The worst of these involved 40-50 prisoners who refused to go back to their cells after two men, who had threatened a governor while lunch was being served, were restrained. All available staff were called to the wing. It was worrying that this was described to the independent monitors by management as a minor incident. Fortunately once order was restored, several officers who were involved in the fracas came to our monthly board meeting that was taking place that morning to tell us what had just happened. One officer said it had been 'absolutely hair-raising' and was only stopped from becoming a major incident that would have needed the Tornado squad by the 'skin of its teeth'. He added: 'If it had occurred at the weekend, I know we wouldn't have had the staff to manage.' Other acts of defiance included a prisoner barricading himself in his cell, another jumping on to the netting between landings, and prisoners smashing the observation panels in their cells.

Lack of staff also resulted in adjudications not being heard. These dealt with offences committed by prisoners while in jail and ranged from possessing illicit substances to violence. Governors were instead rushing from wing to wing to plug gaps in staffing and sometimes doing basic tasks like serving food or filling in forms for new prisoners in Reception. A backlog of fifty adjudications quickly built up. Monitors discovered that to ease their burden adjudications that were over three months old were quietly being dropped. We complained that we didn't feel it was right that prisoners got away with wrongdoing. We were also concerned the lack of adjudications would affect statistics on violence and crime within the prison and give the wrong impression that fewer such incidents were happening than was true.

The time prisoners could interact with each other on a wing was dramatically cut back too. This is important as isolation doesn't help a prisoner re-integrate into society on his release. To save pressure on staff, prisoners were increasingly locked up over lunchtime. Officers began handing over their meal at the cell door, thus intensifying the isolation. The result was that prisoners were spending hours lying on or in bed sleeping the hours away, watching television if they had been allowed one, or just staring at the walls. This did absolutely nothing to help their rehabilitation. It also depressed some prisoners and made others more prone to violence. An officer felt locking prisoners up so frequently gave them too much time to think. 'If they had a difficult problem this was when their black thoughts would take over. All prisoners are broken men before they come in the jail and all have issues of one sort or another.'

Some prisoners complained that when they were unlocked they spent most of the time queuing up to get medication. The frustration of prisoners who were angry at the ongoing lock-ups spilled into violence when they moved along what is known as the spinelink that connects the wings to education and the workshops. There were two violent incidents between January and October 2013 but seven in November 2013 alone. In addition, seven members of staff were injured by prisoners between October and December 2013. Several of them had to go to hospital. Twelve more were treated by prison nursing staff. One prisoner said to me: 'At the end of the day if they treat you like an animal, you will behave like one.'

- - - - - - - -

Lack of staff also affected the keeping of records. Senior officers from the Safer Custody Team responsible for keeping meticulous notes on the use of force and violence between prisoners and between prisoners and staff were regularly cross-deployed round the prison and confessed this important record-keeping was not being done properly. A member of staff subsequently stated that while incidents were noted, detailed records on the use of force were not being kept. It would be wrong if these figures gave a less accurate picture of how bad thing were.

Volunteers at the Citizens Advice Bureau, which operated full-time at the jail and offered valuable help for prisoners about to be released, were frustrated that prisoners with whom they had made appointments to see were locked in their cells, often without notice. Not only was their time wasted going to the wing to be told no one was available but they found the only way they could communicate with inmates was through the locked cell doors which 'goes against our well-established confidentiality policy.'

Staff from the Job Centre Plus workshop who had crucial responsibility for preparing prisoners about to be released reported the lock-downs had a 'massive effect' on the number of prisoners who attended the workshop and therefore an 'adverse effect on our work.' While Working Links, an organisation that gave advice and guidance to people seeking work, also complained that it was difficult to see 'clients' due to staff shortages and lockdowns.

Inevitably the numbers of prisoners taken to the library also slumped. This was a particular shame as they had hours of inactivity in their cells when they could read. It also flew in the face of the Government's reasoning that prisoners didn't need books to be sent to them as they could use the prison library. Monthly forums for foreign nationals and 'mature' prisoners, those over sixty, didn't take place. Wings both inside and out became increasingly grubby and strewn with litter. But, although there were fewer officers available to do time-consuming cell searches, in one month 31 drug caches and 14 mobiles were discovered in one wing.

The new regime was less than a month old when the point was made by someone in authority that if Pentonville, also a category B men's prison in London, could manage the changes, Wormwood Scrubs should be able to do so too. Just a few weeks later in mid-February 2014 a report by the Chief Inspector of Prisons, said that Pentonville would not have a 'viable future' without a major refurbishment and extra staff. He wrote: 'At the time of the inspection (September 2013) the prison was going through a particularly difficult time as it made the transition to new (lower) staffing levels. Nevertheless, it is clear that Pentonville cannot operate as a modern, 21st-century prison without investment in its physical condition, adequate staffing levels to manage its complex population, and effective support from the centre. If these things cannot be provided, considerations should be given to whether HMP Pentonville has a viable future.' The highly critical report brought an immediate response from Michael Spurr, chief executive of the National Offender Management Service, NOMS, who said the jail would receive the support it needed to build on its recent progress.

– – – – – – – –

Four months on it was difficult to find one area of the prison, apart from Security, that hadn't been negatively affected by the changes. One long-serving staffer was in despair: 'The whole regime has been turned upside down. How in the world is it going to be manageable? We are here to keep the prisoners safe and how can we if we don't have enough staff and are not safe ourselves? Prisoners know that and are trying to manipulate the situation.' Only one officer who spoke to me was dismissive of his colleagues: 'The only way to get through the changes is to work together. Some of the senior officers are doing the equivalent of curling up and dying rather than recognising this is a crisis and asking what they can do to help.'

It was also painfully obvious that if prison officers were changing wings on a daily basis and up to three times a day the important relationship between prisoner and staff would disintegrate. If it came to defusing a potentially difficult situation it would be less likely that a prisoner would listen to an officer he didn't know and much more difficult for the officer to build up a connection with the prisoner. It would also be much harder for an officer to recognise when a vulnerable prisoner was depressed or in danger of self-harming, or when a potentially violent prisoner was about to erupt. It was also obviously an enormous challenge for an officer, particularly at a senior level, to go into a wing and deal with many prisoners he had never met and had no time to familiarise himself with. The lack of consistency bothered several. 'Prisoners know when there is no consistency,' said one staff member, 'and they will manipulate that. Although the regime is similar each wing has different prisoners and different staff. Prisoners need to see that the staff are in control, otherwise you are asking for trouble.' Another wondered if anyone at NOMS had asked anyone who actually worked in a prison what they thought before making all the changes. A representative of NOMS told me they had.

A senior officer with 21 years' service was proud that he always worked well with prisoners. 'If staff don't have time to interact with prisoners the rapport will go,' he said. 'It's wrong to depend too much on the goodwill of the prisoner. Time out of cell is important to these guys.' Another long-serving officer had noticed signs that prisoners were less keen to relate to staff. 'It's become like it was in the bad old days twenty years ago and flies right in the face of rehabilitation. How are they going to see another way of life if the only person they talk to is whoever is in their cell and is also committing crimes? I believe prison officers can inspire some criminals, show them that there is another way and perhaps turn a corner.'

This too seemed to fly in the face of what NOMS intended. On 5 February 2013 Michael Spurr, chief executive of NOMS, spoke at the all-party Penal Affairs Parliamentary Group at the House of Commons. He first talked about the 'major programme in prisons to reduce costs, applying the benchmark from competition and introducing new ways of working that will allow us to operate regimes more efficiently, to provide more activity for prisoners, but reduce overall staffing numbers.' He then confirmed his belief in the value of prisoner/prison officer relationships. 'Every contact matters is our mantra now. If we have fewer staff it is even more important that each contact with an individual prisoner is meaningful.'

As well as prisoners having less chance to talk to officers their opportunities to connect with a chaplain were also reduced, partly because the number of chaplains was cut again. This worried some staff who were concerned about the radicalisation of prisoners. 'Which chaplains are now around most to offer the biggest chance of pastoral care? Imams,' said one. 'I wonder how many prisoners are handed a Koran to help them find a little comfort. Where are the C of E and Catholic priests? Not full-time and not around.' This also bothered one of the chaplains. 'It has become very difficult to access prisoners in the wings. If it is lockdown we cannot get the cells opened and if they are upset it is very unsatisfactory to have to speak through the door.'

There was, however, a small sign of recognition that all was not well. After the new regime had been running for a month or so NOMS acknowledged that the staff-cutting it had insisted upon despite warnings from those on the shop floor that the prison couldn't function or be safe with so few staff, had been too radical and that more staff needed to be employed. The cost of the redundancies and payoffs had amounted to over £5million. One management figure said: 'It was not sensible to make people redundant and was done against the advice of governors generally. We are now recruiting to replace some of those people, but the way the system works, it will take several months.'

A long-serving officer criticised this turnaround. 'The voluntary exit departure scheme designed to reduce staff numbers was a terrible mistake. They lost 200 years of experience when just eight staff walked out of the door at Wormwood Scrubs. Their replacements will be paid less and are likely to have five years experience at most. What most worries me about this is that it takes years to know where to draw the line between being friendly with a prisoner and inappropriate behaviour when you get too sucked in. '

The culmination of all the changes took the prison backwards rather than forwards, so much so that I thought the 2002 report on Wormwood Scrubs by Anne Owers, then Chief Inspector of Prisons, could, apart from reference to staff suspensions, have applied to the prison in 2014.

She wrote: 'Problems were compounded by the constant struggle to keep going a regime for which staffing levels had not been agreed, and in the face of staff sickness and suspensions. The prison had lacked the necessary support and direction from Prison Service Headquarters to drive through agreements on appropriate staffing levels. As a result, managers were involved in day to day negotiation about what could be provided and how staff might be redeployed to provide it. Our analysis showed that in two working days, 30% of senior officers and 25% of officers had been cross-deployed and were working in areas with which they were unfamiliar. What prisoners could expect varied from day to day and from wing to wing; managers unfamiliar with a wing depended heavily on basic grade staff for information and sometimes decisions. The absence of accurate monitoring meant that there was no way for senior management to check, let alone influence, real outcomes. There must be agreement on the staffing levels needed to allow the prison to deliver agreed regimes.'

On 1 November, just two weeks after the huge upheaval, young offenders aged between 18 and 21 began arriving at Wormwood Scrubs. The prison was in such turmoil that I wondered whether the planned arrangement might be delayed. It wasn't, partly because Feltham Young Offenders prison in west London, where they would normally have been sent, was in a dire state.

In the spring of 2013 Chief Inspector of Prisons Nick Hardwick said: 'Feltham as a whole is an unacceptably violent place.' He added: 'Despite excellent work in some cases, staff were unable to prevent a high number of very concerning incidents that carried a significant risk of serious injury. Staff were sometimes overwhelmed by the challenges they face.' He told BBC Radio 4's Today programme: 'If you were a parent with a child in Feltham, you'd be terrified.'

Levels of violence in Feltham reached such a pitch that something had to be done to avoid serious consequences, including, I was told, the possibility of murder. Most of the violence was gang-related. On one occasion a group of ten inmates stomped on a youth's head until he was unconscious. There were also concerns about the mounting level of self-harming. It was arranged that Wormwood Scrubs and other London prisons would take between 50 and 100 of these youths. Staff worried how they would cope. 'Feltham has a ratio of staffing that is 1:10,' one said. 'The Prison Service is putting young adults into adult prisons without any extra resources to enable us to cope.'

There are several stipulations about looking after 18 – 21-year olds in an adult prison. One of these is that they must not share a cell with an adult. This posed some problems as Wormwood Scrubs was nearly full to capacity at the time. It was also a fact that younger prisoners tended to self-harm and be involved in assault incidents more often than older prisoners. The younger the prison population the more propensity there was for violence.

The first few arrivals caused problems straight away by being abusive and using foul language, especially to female staff. One flooded his cell, another challenged an officer to tell him what he could do to be banned from the jail. When he was told there was nothing, he stated that he would kick the officer every day until it happened. Another swore at a senior female officer, then threatened to rape her. A third went on a dirty protest and then started tearing down the ceiling of his cell. Several of them had to be taken to the Segregation Unit because of their violence, which must have been very destabilising for teenagers. I saw a few of them when they were allowed out for some exercise in the adjacent yard swaggering, chatting and laughing. They looked quite at home but apparently how they behaved was not necessarily how they felt.

'They can't cope in an adult jail,' I was told. 'It runs very differently from a young offenders unit and they get much less attention. They are okay when they are showing off to their peer group, but they behave quite differently once they are on their own and are at serious risk of self harming or suicide.' Fortunately an arrangement was in place that if an adult jail did prove too difficult for any of them they would be taken back to Feltham at any time of the day or night.

The problem is, said another officer, 'they have men's bodies but kids' brains. They have no idea what is and isn't appropriate behaviour. They are also used to being controlled by a gang that has a rigid hierarchy and if they are told to whack someone they will do it without asking any questions. The older prisoners are already fed up to the teeth with them. Every time they assault another member of a different gang, maybe from east or west London, everyone in the wing is banged up, which annoys them, but we just have to stop the young ones from killing each other.'

A firm idea of what to do with these difficult inmates came from an officer with more than twenty years' experience of working in prisons. 'They are so immature they shouldn't be in places like this. They should go to boot camp when they leave school for two years minimum. I am sure they could set them up at military bases. There is much too much of asking them how they are, instead of setting boundaries and being disciplined.'

There were some signs that setting boundaries might work. When they became violent on the wings three officers used Control and Restraint measures which immobilised their bodies with prescribed and controlled movements.

'The first time it happened they were completely shocked and yelled: "You can't do that," ' I was told. 'We told them we could. After that most of them began to behave.'

Fortunately there is hope that things may change. In early July 2014 Michael Spurr, Chief Executive of National Offenders Management Service (NOMS) finally voiced his concern on BBC2's Newsnight programme about the increase in the number of suicides in prison. He added: 'We've ended up with fewer staff than needed.' It is something governors, prison officers and independent monitors have said continuously since 2010. It is a great pity that it has taken so long for NOMS to realise the obvious.

Nor will it happen quickly. The way the Prison Service operates it takes around five months to recruit new officers.

EPILOGUE

I wrote this book because I felt it was important that the wider community had some sense of what a prison was like. Spending significant amounts of time in Wormwood Scrubs over nearly ten years has had a profound effect on me. Initially, I felt those who had committed crimes should be punished, locked up, not have television or PlayStation, or be allowed to loaf about all day. I now know being locked up for the greater part of every day with or without television rots the brain and drains the body. Offenders need to be stretched in every way and, apart from the mentally ill, should be made to get up and do something, even if it involves rewashing floors and repainting walls. They need structure and routine.

It is equally important for them to learn to read and write and imperative they take responsibility for their own lives. Unless prisoners draw something positive from the prison experience that makes them want to change, they will continue to offend. This is in the public interest as it will help reduce the number of future victims.

I also had no idea that prison was society's scrapyard for those with mental disorders and/or addictions whom the country at large would prefer to forget about. Prison isn't the right place for them. Prison is also a place full of personal tragedies. Many inmates have been so abused and neglected that they have never had a chance to do well. Nor can they develop normal personal relationships. When they leave prison they can't cope with the outside world and go on to commit more crime. It is not a coincidence that there were 50 per cent more suicides in prisons in 2014 than the previous year. The number of assaults in adult male prisons also increased by a similar proportion.

I don't pretend there are easy answers to the problems of running prisons especially when the Ministry of Justice has had to make more than its fair share of cuts since 2010. But I do have thoughts of my own about some possible long-term solutions that could ease the pressure on a big prison. I don't believe foreign nationals should be detained in overcrowded London prisons when they could be housed in specialist institutions like Huntercombe Prison in Oxfordshire, which is a dedicated site for them. This would concentrate UK Border Agency resources and make it easier to remove the prisoners at the end of their sentences. Deportations should also be handled more quickly. I believe a country's right to get rid of criminals who arrived illegally outweighs that individual's right to a family life. Genuine asylum seekers are an exception.

I don't believe that the Coalition is correct in wanting to build ever-larger prisons. They are notoriously difficult to run and usually rely on a lot of inexperienced staff. Instead, the money allocated for such 'titan' prisons should be used to build secure units for the mentally ill and addicts where they can be properly treated rather than merely housed.

I don't think prisons, of all places, should operate a strange collusion with drug addicts to keep them dosed up with methadone. If the Human Rights Act gives individuals the right to take drugs, prisons should surely have the right to state they don't endorse an illegal act even when it involves a class A substitute drug.

Without foreign nationals, addicts and the mentally ill, prisons would be more manageable and able to focus properly on rehabilitation.

I believe that the administration and bureaucracy in prisons should be urgently addressed. Instead of employing vast numbers of civil servants to create ever increasing convoluted and verbally inflated prison service orders, individuals should be employed who can write or edit in a concise, easy to understand way that will shorten them without affecting security or safety. This will help lighten the bureaucratic burden on staff and cut down on repetitive form filling which takes up so much time. It would be a sensible way of cutting down on numbers without affecting their duties with prisoners.

In addition superfluous army barracks should be converted into boot camps where former military personnel could try to give dysfunctional youths discipline, boundaries and structure. Teenage years are a time of change and giving difficult young men goals and motivation could set them on a more constructive path.

Sweden has tried to find the elusive balance between humanity and security in the way it treats prisoners and their reoffending rates are half those of the UK. They also give substantial post-prison support. We need to do more of that in the UK. Even those inmates who change their attitude in prison are at a loss without routine and structure when they come out. They need a proper place to live, a mentor they can rely on and most of all self-belief that they can turn themselves around.

In chapter three I mentioned John McCarthy, Governor of Wormwood Scrubs, who wrote a letter to The Times in November 1981 describing himself as 'the manager of a large penal dustbin'. I was powerfully reminded of his letter following the shambles of the cutbacks and regime change in October 2013. Sadly his words seem just as relevant today, 33 years later.

He wrote: *'I did not join the Prison Service to manage overcrowded cattle pens, nor did I join to run a prison where the interests of the individuals have to be sacrificed continually to the interests of the institution, nor did I join to be a member of a service where the staff that I admire are forced to run a society that debases... as it is evident that the present uncivilised conditions in prison are likely to continue and as I find this incompatible with any moral ethic, I wish to give notice that I as governor of the major prison in the United Kingdom cannot for any longer tolerate either as a professional or as an individual the inhumanity of the system within which I work.'*

Most of all governments of all political parties should try to do better than merely applying a sticking plaster to a rupturing artery.

THE END

ACKNOWLEDGEMENTS

I would like to thank fellow members of the IMB
and the staff at Wormwood Scrubs who,
despite many obstacles do the best the best job they
can, John Reiss and his team at Premier PR,
my agent Robert Smith, Martin Colyer for designing
the book and my husband Robert Low for his
patience and good advice. And always my children.

Printed in Great Britain
by Amazon